196894

D1471103

Sensory Play

Play in the EYFS

Fully revised and updated to reflect the 2012 EYFS

Contents

For Freya and Zach, for teaching me all they know about sensory play.

Published by Practical Pre-School Books , A Division of MA Education Ltd,
St Jude's Church, Dulwich Road, Herne Hill, London, SE24 0PB. Tel 020 7738 5454
www.practicalpreschoolbooks.com

© MA Education Ltd 2011. Revised edition 2013.

Illustrated by Cathy Hughes. Front cover photos clockwise from left: © iStockphoto.com/DBTN,
© iStockphoto.com/jstroh, © MA Education Ltd/Lucie Carlier, © Sue Gascoyne 2011.

Play in the EYFS: Sensory Play ISBN: 978-1-909280-30-4

Introducing sensory play

What is sensory play?

Imagine a walk in the woods; a visit to the seaside; a child mixing and splodging paint with a fat brush, or better still their fingers; or building with smooth wooden blocks. What do these all have in common? Each experience is inextricably linked to the senses. For example, the woodland walk conjures up crunching leaves underfoot while dappled light casts on tree trunks ripe for climbing. A trip to the seaside offers the satisfaction of shaping wet sand, creating channels for frothing water and the taste of salty air. Painting gives the pleasure and cold silky feel of paint or the visual explosion of colour as shades mix and loop. Block play offers the opportunity to create imaginary castles with cool wooden blocks satisfyingly clinking. The essence of the experience is both captured and conveyed through the colour and lights, sounds, feel, warmth, smells and taste.

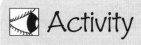

Activity

Try to imagine a vivid childhood play memory. Was one or more of your senses really prominent? What do you think makes it so vivid? How does it make you feel?

Compare these experiences to the visual focus and passive nature of watching television or playing computer games – just two of the trends in 21st century play cited in a recent research project (Sue Gascoyne, January 2010). Or visit the average toy shop, with shelf upon shelf of brightly coloured toys, some of which flash, bleep or talk, and the visual (and to a lesser extent auditory) focus of many toys is apparent. Opportunities for children to actually touch or taste are often discouraged, or limited to plastic. Play now primarily takes place indoors, where temperatures are constant, and smells and environmental sounds masked. All this contributes to play where sensory experience is limited. Contrast this with the vivid childhood play memories you may have of running barefoot through grass, making mud pies and rose petal perfume and the appeal of multi-sensory play is evident.

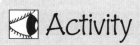

Activity

For a reminder of the sensory limitations of plastic, close your eyes and place your hand in a bag of brightly coloured plastic toys. As the visual stimulus is removed, the appeal and 'differentness' of these toys quickly disappears.

For something so fundamental to children's growth and development, definitions of sensory play itself are remarkably elusive! Sensory play is essentially play that engages one or more of the senses. As such, most play clearly has the potential to be sensory. Sensory play differs to other types of play in that the sensory focus adds a significant and integral extra dimension to the play. Usher (2010) defines

sensory play as "*play that provides opportunities for children ... to use all their senses, or play that encourages the use of one particular sense*". Sensory play is commonly accessed in the outdoor environment, and some forms, like sand and water play, can be intrinsically messy – although this is something for us adults to embrace rather than dread! As the previous examples amply show, many sensory-rich play opportunities surround us in our everyday lives, without costing a penny. Most children are hardwired to know how to 'do' sensory play and need no instructions when faced with sand, mud or water. Rather it is us adults who may have lost sight of the awe and wonder that such open-ended materials offer, the limitless possibilities and opportunities for quiet reflection, and the fact that some mess or even the momentary appearance of disorder (it is perfectly natural for children to combine objects and resources), is definitely worth the effort. The essential ingredients of quality play have been identified by some as space, time and materials. When it comes to sensory play this is all the more important as children need to be given the space, time, and permission to truly experience the sensory-rich qualities of materials.

Our amazing senses

If asked about our senses, most people would probably cite the five senses of sight, smell, sound, touch and taste. Although these external senses are vital, as we will discover in chapter two, the lesser-known but crucially important inner or 'sixth' senses detect position, balance, movement, and more. Similarly, when we think of our senses, our eyes, ears and nose spring to mind, but really our whole body is a sensory organ as the skin around our sense organs, such as the inner ear, is packed with receptors to detect touch, pressure, heat, cold and pain. From birth, babies' senses are tuned to detecting touch, space, their mother's smell, voice and repeated sounds. Hughes gives the example of a baby who had already grown accustomed to the theme tune of Coronation Street from exposure in the womb and on hearing it as a newborn, turned towards the sound and "suddenly became alert and responsive" (Anita Hughes, 2006, p.18).

Processing sensory information

Every sensory experience provides the foundations upon which all subsequent knowledge, thought and creativity are based. Each time a child (or indeed an adult) encounters a sensory stimulus, a neuron (brain cell) connects to another neuron, establishing new connections in the brain. Signals flow along these complex neural networks, from one neuron to another, allowing the brain cells to communicate with each other by relaying information about emotions as well as everything we see, hear, taste, touch and smell. Each new sensory stimulus adds to the network, while repeated experiences increase the thickness and strength of the connections, helping signals to travel faster (Nancy Wartik & LaVonne Carlson-Finnerty, 1993). In this way each of us will develop a unique network of nerve connections created from our own unique sensory experiences, which means that "*the richer our sensory experiences the more intricate will be the patterns for learning, thought and creativity*" (Carla Hannaford, 1995, p.30).

Returning to that walk in the woods, when we hear the word 'woods' all our experiences relating to woods come to mind (see Diagram 1). Be it climbing trees, the feeling of achievement having balanced on a fallen log, feeling the texture of bark, scrunching leaves, looking up through the leaf canopy or walking through leaf litter. Memories of the rush of air on the face and scent of the forest while cycling through a wooded glade, the thrill of playing hide and seek or being chased, the exhilaration of swinging on a rope or warmth of dappled light. Smelling moss and rotting leaves, foraging for fungi, the satisfaction of peeling away rotten bark and revealing scurrying woodlice, intricate patterns made by the sun and leaves, the sound of bird song and so on. All these different sensory-rich experiences can potentially be accessed from the word 'woods'. Broad-based knowledge depends upon a multitude of separate multi-sensory images and memories, developed and reshaped from a wealth of separate, yet interlinked, sensory experiences. Without the unique sensory experiences and memories that we attach to words, they would lack resonance and real meaning. Thus someone can only truly

Diagram 1: Just some of the different sensory experiences
a walk in the woods can offer

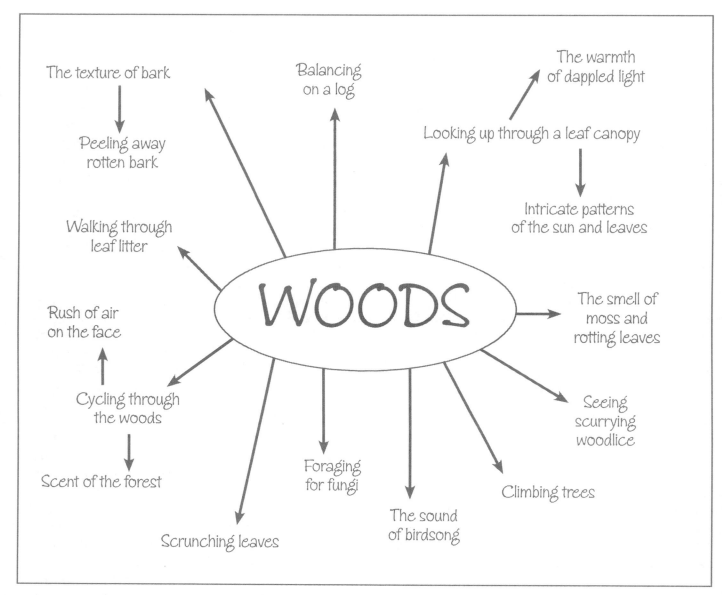

The texture of bark → Peeling away rotten bark

Balancing on a log

The warmth of dappled light

Looking up through a leaf canopy → Intricate patterns of the sun and leaves

Walking through leaf litter

Rush of air on the face

Cycling through the woods → Scent of the forest

WOODS

The smell of moss and rotting leaves

Seeing scurrying woodlice

Climbing trees

Foraging for fungi

The sound of birdsong

Scrunching leaves

Table 1: Examples of sensory-rich play

Sand	A treasure basket – a basket of natural and household objects
Water, bubbles, ice	Pastry, playdough, plasticine etc.
Pebbles and shells	Leaves, twigs, moss etc.
Shaving foam, gloop, paint	String, fabric, buttons etc.
Mud	Dried rice, pasta, couscous, lentils and seeds etc.

understand snow by actually feeling it themselves. No amount of stories and pictures will convey its essence or replace the magic of encountering snow first hand.

 Activity

Imagine describing snow, ice, or couscous to a visitor from another world for whom words have limited meaning. See how difficult it is to do, how many different words you need to use and how far the visitor is from understanding the sensation of touching these first-hand.

Tapping into this amazing connectivity, richness and immediacy of thought is key to bringing a curriculum to life. As we shall discover in chapter five, the senses can help make learning relevant and real. The Statutory Framework for the EYFS highlights the need for explorative play, active learning and critical thinking, recognising the importance of *"igniting children's curiosity and enthusiasm for learning, and for building their capacity to learn and to thrive"* (Department for Education, July 2011, p.5). Crowe recognises that *"without meaning words are useless ... words are connectors ... children's senses cry out to be used first to provide the experiences that they will later need in order to connect. Children must feel their world, listen to it, see it, taste it, smell it, 'know' it...That takes time and a great deal of silent investigation in peace and privacy"* (Brenda Crowe, 1983, p.39). We return to focussed investigations in chapter three, as children explore unusual natural objects with sand and water.

Different parts of the brain are associated with different functions and are broadly responsible for processing different sensory information from the eyes, ears etc. But as we shall discover in chapter two this does not happen in isolation. The brain integrates all of the different pieces of information in order to make sense of the world. Experiments have shown just how powerful the different senses are in ultimately decoding experiences. For example,

 Activity

Try the experiment opposite yourself by adding food colour or flavourings to drinks to see if it changes other people's perceptions of taste. **Always check allergies first.**

Diagram 2: Explaining sensory stimulus (adapted from McIntyre, C. 2010, p.87)

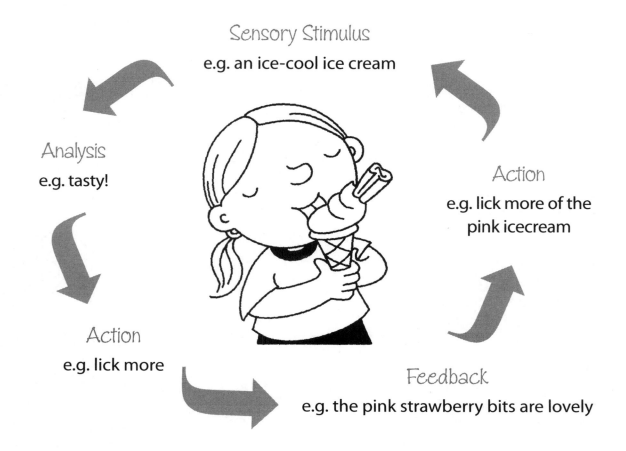

Sensory Stimulus
e.g. an ice-cool ice cream

Analysis
e.g. tasty!

Action
e.g. lick more of the
pink icecream

Action
e.g. lick more

Feedback
e.g. the pink strawberry bits are lovely

a group of participants was given berry-coloured drink to taste (which was actually lemon or peppermint flavoured) and were convinced that the drink was berry-flavoured because that's what their eyes had prepared them to expect. If you have ever drunk from a cup and discovered that something wasn't quite what you expected, but you couldn't pinpoint a flavour, this could be an example of feedback from each sense causing confusion.

When a child learns something, the information from the environment gained through their senses travels through the central nervous system to the brain to be analysed. A message is sent to the appropriate part of the body and results in an action. If operating efficiently, a cycle develops between the sensory stimulus, mind and body, with feedback from each stage forming a fundamental part of the learning process (Christine Macyntyre, 2010, p.87). See Diagram 2 above for an example of the sensory stimulus cycle. Some children with special educational needs (SEN) experience problems when a lack of feedback makes it difficult to learn from situations and therefore they repeat the same mistakes.

Others experience difficulties when the senses do not all act together as they should – known as sensory integration. As we shall see in the SEN chapter (p.46), an understanding of a child's needs and lots of fun, targeted sensory activities, can help to address this syndrome.

Theories of sensory play

Although our understanding of the brain is still evolving the origins of sensory play can be traced through the teachings of numerous theorists. Although no one individual stands out as championing sensory play, the importance of sensorial experiences and environments can be seen in the work of several theorists. As early as the 1600s John Comenius recommended sensory experiences rather than formal teaching for children. He is credited with introducing a visual focus to learning by adding illustrations to books. In the 1800s Johann Pestalozzi emphasised the importance of the senses and basing learning on things that are familiar to children, much of the beauty of sensory-rich play.

Friedrich Froebel (1782-1852) placed an emphasis upon sensory play and first-hand experience as a tool for learning, principles that were reflected in his kindergarten.

Rudolph Steiner (1861-1925) recognised that children learn from the people and environment that surround them. Steiner settings are characterised therefore by an emphasis upon natural open-ended materials which children can explore at their own pace, like the nature tables described in chapter three.

Maria Montessori (1870-1952) believed that children learn best through their senses, a central focus of Montessori practice today. She argued that children have 'sensitive periods' when their senses are ready to learn new ideas and that if we spot these we can best support children's development. She suggested that children's senses come first in their intellect and that adults have a role to play in offering and arranging an interesting and attractive environment for children. She recognised the importance of providing appropriate materials and giving children adequate time and space to experiment, key roles that we will return to in chapter six.

Susan Isaacs (1885-1948) saw the value of "free, unfettered play" and how with appropriate adult support children can make sense of the world themselves. She recognised that *"no experimental scientist has a greater thirst for new facts than an ordinary, healthy, active child"* and examples of this type of play and the importance of children being given opportunities to play is a key tool in adding to children's knowledge of the world (Linda Pound, 2006, p.33).

Jean Piaget (1896-1980) believed that a child's interactions with their environment create learning. The first stage in a child's development, the sensori-motor stage, draws heavily on sensory experiences. Occurring in the first two years of life, it is characterised by most learning occurring through the senses and manipulation of objects. Piaget introduced the term 'disequilibrium' when a child encounters something unexpected and needs to assimilate and accommodate this new

information and learning. Like Dewey, Piaget suggested that children's 'curiosity drives their learning' (Carol G. Mooney, 2000, p.62) and that through symbolic play, such as making an imaginary meal from pebbles, they make sense of objects and the world. Piaget believed that babies need to manipulate and explore objects and that these objects should be interesting. This has clear parallels with a treasure basket, a selection of 'treasures' picked for their unusual qualities and perfect for exploration.

The very design of space in Reggio Emilia pre-schools maximises opportunities for sensory awareness. Children are able to gain "an awareness of scale, colour, texture, sound, smell, light, micro-climate" (Bishop in Abbot and Nutbrown, 2006, p.78) by virtue of the arrangement of space, use of mirrors, variety of transparency, reflectance, colour, texture and acoustic qualities that they encounter. This exploration of different materials is further extended by the use of professional artists in Reggio settings.

Theories of heuristic play, treasure baskets, loose parts

Working in orphanages in rural Italy in the 1940s Elinor Goldschmied observed babies' fascination for playing with household objects, like those found in a kitchen. From her observations of babies playing, the idea of a Treasure Basket – a basket of natural and household objects for babies aged seven to twelve months, was born. In the 1980s the term 'heuristic play', meaning discovery play, was coined by Goldschmied and Anita Hughes. This involved exploratory play with lots of bags of different objects, e.g. bags of jam jar lids, curtain hoops, etc. (Elinor Goldschmied and Sonia Jackson, 1994). This type of play was felt to be particularly suited to two-year-olds exploring their newly discovered mobility and independence. Research and observations of older children have since highlighted the value of treasure baskets for children aged six months to six years and even older, as well as children with special educational needs (Sue Gascoyne, 2009). 'Loose parts' is the term coined by architect Simon Nicholson in the 1970s for open-ended materials such as sand, sticks, balls, cardboard boxes, crates, shells, pallets, gravel, pine cones, logs, pebbles, containers and guttering that can be used in limitless ways. The potential for creativity has close parallels to treasure baskets and heuristic play, albeit on a larger scale.

Theories of brain development

Brierley (1994) understood the importance of pattern and variety in engaging the infant's brain. This still rings true but research into the workings of the brain, and especially in babies and young children, has changed understanding dramatically since then. In particular it is now believed that although the early years remain a vital stage in brain development, the brain does not stop growing at six years of age, its 'plasticity' (ability to change) continues throughout our lives, peaking in infancy and adolescence. 'Sensitive periods' have replaced the emphasis upon 'critical windows' of development, in recognition of the brain's amazing ability

Theories of sensory-rich play outdoors

Since much sensory play is freely available in the outdoor environment and noise and mess are less of a factor, it is also worth mentioning some of the pioneers of outdoor play. With a focus on health, Margaret McMillan's practice strongly encouraged play and rest outdoors. Susan Isaacs also recognised the benefits to exploration and enquiry from play outdoors. In 1995 Forest Schools were established in the UK, with children being given the opportunity to explore woodland environments. Following the model established in Denmark, the Forest School movement has taken hold in the UK, capturing children's and adults' hearts and minds. More recently lack of access to nature and the outdoor environment has been described as 'nature deficit disorder' (Richard Louv, 2005). While positive benefits from even looking at green views, let alone experiencing them first-hand, have also been discovered (e.g. *American Journal of Public Health*, September 2004; Jo Barton et al., 2010).

to evolve (ESRC, 2007). The division of the brain in terms of function is another factor that we now understand more fully, with different parts of the brain able to adapt and take on functions not previously thought possible, as we shall discover in chapter two. However, the links between neuroscience and education remain largely undiscovered.

As this brief skim through the key shapers of play has revealed, the importance of the senses and value of sensory-rich experiences has long been recognised as an underlying element of play theory.

The benefits of sensory play

As we have already learnt, sensory-rich experiences are great for brain development in babies through to adults. Neuroscientists have also identified a strong link between memory recollections and the sight, smell and touch senses. If you've ever encountered a particular smell, good or bad, that has brought memories flooding back, then you will have experienced this first-hand. Sensory-rich play is an inclusive way of encouraging learning and development, as the hands-on approach appeals to children with different thinking and learning styles. Sensory activities help bring learning to life generally, but will particularly benefit children with SEN, those with English as an additional language and those who enjoy a practical approach, especially boys. The open-ended nature of sensory-rich play (in that there are no 'right' or 'wrong' ways of playing) means that this type of play provides an inclusive learning opportunity with plenty of potential for developing problem solving, exploration and creativity. Sensory-rich play resources each have their own distinct properties or ways of 'behaving' for children to explore and enjoy. Given time children discover through their own independent learning that sand poured into a sieve will naturally flow through the holes, unless of course water is added to the sand to change

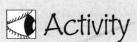 Activity

When adults look at an object like a wooden spoon, we often see it for what it is, i.e. a spoon is a spoon. Children's thinking tends to be less constrained, so a wooden spoon has the potential to be a magic wand, musical beater, talking stick, sword etc. Try to come up with as many different uses as possible for simple objects like a pastry brush, wooden spoon or plug. E.g. a pastry brush could be a tickling stick, a paintbrush, microphone or mini broom. These can be fun, unusual, silly or serious, but try to think of at least 20 different ideas for each object. This fun activity helps recapture some of children's awe and wonder and gives us a taste of how they see the world.

its consistency, as the children in chapter five discover! The appeal for children lies perhaps in the countless opportunities and challenges provided by such simple resources, particularly when combined with their own bodies, or another object or resource. The human brain thrives on variety, stimulation and the unexpected. For children, play with sensory-rich resources offers just that. Open-ended materials, from a cardboard box to sand, paint, pebbles or a treasure basket, enable children (and adults) to represent their experiences, ideas and imagination.

Appraising sensory provision – where do we start?

As we shall discover in chapter three and six, opportunities for sensory play lie all around us, often limited only by adult's attitude and imagination. A starting point in appraising sensory provision in your own setting is to consider the following three factors – environment, yourself and children:

 The environment

The simplest and most natural of environments provide potentially rich environments for sensory play. Throughout the book opportunities for appraising the sensory environment are highlighted by a tree symbol.

Questions to consider:

- Are any senses particularly well-catered for?
- Are any senses currently under stimulated?
- Could the sensory environment be improved with simple actions?

 Yourself

It is important for us to understand our own attitudes to sensory play, get in touch with any childhood play memories and appreciate through hands-on exploration,

some of the child-like wonder of sensory-rich experiences to best support children's play. The eye symbol throughout the book, highlights activities for increasing understanding of our own attitudes and role.

Questions to consider:

- Do you have any particular sensory preferences?
- Does the existing provision favour your own sensory preferences?
- Does your own attitude, experience, or 'phobias' currently limit sensory-rich play?

 Children

By talking with, listening to and observing children playing and simply 'being' we can gain an understanding of their sensory preferences and any sensitivities or difficulties that they may experience. Look out for the face symbols, particularly in chapter four, as these will help improve understanding of children's individual sensory needs.

Questions to consider:

- Do individual children prefer particular sensory experiences?
- Do individual children avoid particular sensory experiences?
- How can you best support all children's sensory needs?

 Continuous provision

The sensory environment is not static but ever changing. It makes sense to continuously review provision and needs rather than viewing a sensory appraisal as a one-off process. This also provides an opportunity to appraise the final aspect of any audit, that of assessing the impacts of any actions taken. Look out for the mini trowel symbol, particularly in chapters two and three, to signpost sensory-rich activity ideas for you to try.

It is scarcely imaginable for us to think about life without our senses. Using the analogy of a windowless, lightless house with solid metal walls and roof we can picture our sense organs as windows, through which we discover the world and ourselves. With no contact with the outside world, it would be like having no sense organs to know what is happening inside or around us (Sarah Riedman, 1962, p.13). The importance of sensory-rich experiences cannot be over emphasised in providing the source of all learning and enriching our daily lives. To better understand this, this chapter introduces the brain and each of the senses, explaining how they work and providing ideas for increasing sensory stimulation.

The brain

The cortex is the softly folded outer surface of the brain that many of us will think of when we hear the word brain. About 3mm thick and covering about $2000cm^2$, in area, the cortex is formed from about 10 million nerve cells (John Brierely, 1994). Each neuron is made up of a brain cell with tendril-like branches called dendrites at one end, and a length of axon and branch-like synapses at the other. The function of the dendrites is to receive chemical signals from other synapses, thereby establishing connections. Beneath the grey outer surface of the neurons is a white pulpy layer formed from millions of axons. The cortex is divided into two distinct halves, left and right hemisphere, which give it its distinct walnut-like appearance. The left half primarily focuses on

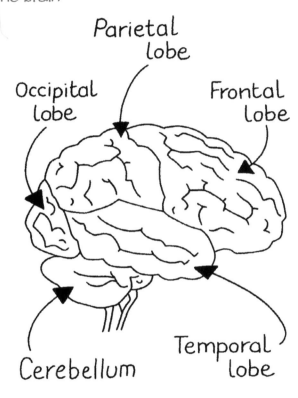

Diagram 3: The 4 lobes of the brain

speech and movement and the right visual patterns, but this is to oversimplify its complexity. The two sides of the brain are connected by the corpus callosum, a thick band of nerves which enables the two halves to work in perfect harmony.

Table 2: Different senses

External senses	Internal senses
Visual (sight)	Vestibular (balance)
Olfactory (smell)	Proprioceptive (position in space)
Auditory (sound)	Kinaesthetic (movement)
Tactile (touch)	Baric (weight)
Gustatory (taste)	Thermic (temperature)

Each hemisphere has four lobes (shown in diagram 3), the temporal (associated with memory and auditory skills); occipital at the rear of the head (responsible for visual processing); parietal (associated with integrating information and mathematical skills); and frontal lobe (the area behind the forehead associated with cognitive thinking and movement.) In addition different parts of the cortex are 'specialised' for hearing, taste, smell, touch, sight and movement. Beneath the cortex at the rear of the head lies the cerebellum. This deeply ridged area is described by Breirely as the 'automatic pilot'. It is responsible for habituated actions, that is things that once learnt we don't need to think about, like walking, handwriting etc. Deep within the brain is the limbic system including the thalamus – the central 'switchboard' for receiving and analysing all sensations.

Starting with the external senses, most developed at birth, we will begin our tour of the senses.

Olfactory (smell)

The sense of smell is one of our most under-used senses and yet together with the sense of touch, the most developed at birth. Not surprisingly perhaps smell and touch (both linked to the oldest limbic part of the brain) are very strongly associated with childhood memories and emotion. Forbes (2004) reports research carried out at the John Radcliffe Maternity Unit in the 1970s where breast milk was soaked onto pads and the babies responded only to their mother's milk, by turning their head towards the familiar scent.

Our smell receptors are located in our nostrils and unlike all the other senses, feedback from these does not cross hemispheres, so a smell sensed in the left nostril travels to the left side of the brain for analysis. It's difficult to imagine, but our nose contains about 10 million smell receptors made up of 20 different types, each responsible for detecting a different type of smell (Olga Bogdashina, 2003). The sense of smell is inextricably linked to the sense of taste, as we are all too aware of when we have a cold and food can taste non-descript or bland.

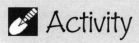 ## Activity

As one of our most underused senses it is important for us to provide fun ways of increasing smell stimulation. Babies and children will enjoy playing this smelly game!

Gather some clean odd socks or mini organza bags, cotton wool pads and a range of different herbs, spices, flavoured oils and smelly substances like coffee, fruit tealeaves, vanilla pods, lavender, cinnamon sticks and cloves. Put a little of each smelly item in a sock or bag (for the liquids add drops to the cotton wool instead). Tie the socks/bags securely with ribbon or string before offering to babies and children to smell. With babies, introduce each smell one at a time to avoid sensory overload and to understand more about their likes and dislikes. Do so by gently stroking their legs, toes or arm, so that the smell slowly wafts to their nose. Let the baby discover the smell and watch closely to see their reaction. If appropriate talk about each smell as the baby explores. Take it in turns smelling the sock/bag and accentuate your reactions - "Mmm that smells lovely", or "Aargh, that's pongy".

When selecting items for a treasure basket be sure to think about the sense of smell and select items that will appeal to this sense, e.g. metal, leather, a shell, lavender bag, fresh lemon, lime or orange – pricked first with a fork.

With older children invite them to guess what each smell is (possibly by matching word or picture cards) to each smell. Use to inspire smelly stories or games. Allow older children to open up the socks/bags to discover what each smell 'looks like'. Talk about what they are, where they come from, how they're used, what they like or dislike and if they remind them of anything.

Offer a selection of smelly substances/foods for older children to explore smelly art or collage. Coffee, fruity tea bags and normal tea could work well.

Tactile (touch)

Our skin is the sensory organ responsible for the sense of touch. One of the first senses to develop even before birth, within the layers of skin are located five different types

Crucial to everyday life is what Ayres (Ayres A. Jean, 1972) described as 'habituation' when a feeling or sensation fades and becomes accepted as a habit. For most of us the sensation of wearing clothes quickly fades after we get dressed. But for some children with sensory processing difficulties, this is not the case and these sensations continue to have an invasive sensory presence in everyday life.

Activity

For many young children the home can present a multitude of opportunities to touch and explore and yet many of these may be discouraged and forbidden (some rightly so for safety reasons). In these crucial early years it is vital for babies and young children to be given ample opportunities to experience the world through touch. Offer a treasure basket of natural and household objects for children to discover a world in a basket. (See 'Sensory play in action' (p.17) for guidance).

Visual (sight)

Although not the most developed sense at birth, our visual sense is the most stimulated sense, with 80% of all stimulation visual, making it probably the most important of the external senses. Our brains are hardwired to search for pattern and variety. Yet as we've already noted, most children's toys typically stimulate the visual sense above all others. Indeed, take away the bright colours from most plastic toys and unless they have added sounds, children are offered very little in the way of sensory appeal. Within its quest for pattern, babies' brains are programmed to recognise the features of a face, something even newborn babies can do. Although not fully developed, the eyes are already ingeniously 'programmed' to focus best at an adult arm's length, the distance between a carers face and a feeding baby.

of receptors to detect pressure, heat, cold , pain and light touch. Some of these are found just beneath the outer dead layer of the epidermis, while others are found deep within the dermis layer of the skin. Touch receptors are not evenly distributed across the body, with the majority located in the mouth, lips and hands. The importance of the mouth and hands are apparent when watching a young baby playing with a treasure basket. Most objects accidentally, then purposefully selected will ultimately end up being mouthed, this being the area in which most touch receptors are located. Similarly, when older children encounter an object with which they are unfamiliar and their usual investigation sheds little light, they may ultimately resort to mouthing the object to try to discover what it is.

Activity

Put some brightly coloured plastic toys in a bag and close your eyes while you explore them with your hands. Think about what words come to mind when you feel the toys. Now compare with an eclectic mix of objects (typical of those found in a treasure basket, e.g. a plug, wooden spoon, teaspoon, whisk etc). How do the two sets of objects feel different? Which is more interesting and appealing and why?

Our eyes are the sense organ responsible for vision and their function is to receive and channel light into the nerve endings in the retina at the back of the eye. The images projected by each lens, appear upside down before being inverted and made sense of by the brain. This is not the only instance in which the brain 'translates' the sensory information relayed by the eyes. As each eye covers a slightly different visual field and sees objects from a slightly different angle, it is the brain that has the task of combining the images and making sense of them including filling in any missing gaps, vital for everyday functioning. This same 'skill', together with the preconceived ideas that we all bring to experiences, can be responsible for so-called 'tricks of the eye'. The sensory information then passes to the visual processing part of the brain, located at the back of the head, where different types of information, like colour, shape, size, distance and movement are analysed by different parts of the brain.

When we think of the sense of sight, our eyes are the obvious sensory organ, but in fact without the sophisticated processes at work in the brain we would effectively be blind. This is why it is possible to have perfectly functioning eyes but not be able to see because the connections within the brain have not been established. As noted in the introduction, advances in neuroscience have replaced an emphasis upon 'critical' windows of development – where experiences must take place if development is not to be disadvantaged with a focus now on 'sensitive' time. This recognises the plasticity of the brain, which continues growing, albeit at a lesser pace, throughout adulthood. Characterised by a remarkable ability to adapt in the event of illness, injury or changes in environmental or emotional context, different parts of the brain can evolve to fulfil functions of other parts of the brain. However, early diagnosis of visual (and auditory) processing problems and treatment, e.g. an eye patch for a lazy eye, or corneal or cochlea implant, will greatly increase children's chances of being able to see or hear fully.

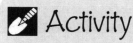

Activity

Introduce fun visualising activities to increase interconnectivity in the brain and to reinforce the connections associated with sight. Use in times of relaxation by inviting children to imagine they are playing at the seaside/in the wood etc and to get them to think about the sorts of sights, sounds and smells they might experience.

So sophisticated are the workings of the brain that true analogies are simplistic and flawed, but like the example of a digital camera, whose memory card is packed with vivid, memory-rich images, it is only when plugged into a computer hard-drive that those images come to life. Similarly, with careful editing, the image can be cropped, air brushed and moulded, just as the brain fills the gaps in the sensory information provided by the eyes to create the final image that we see. Parallels can also be drawn in terms of how the images are stored and retrieved. As we discovered in chapter one, each word or image ultimately links to a wealth of sensory-rich experiences that we readily retrieve through association and memory. Similarly our system (or lack of one) for archiving the mountain of digital images that many of us accrue is crucial to their rapid retrieval!

As connections in the brain develop, with time these are myelinated (or insulated) to enable electrical signals to pass from one neuron to another quicker and more efficiently. The nerve fibres carrying information from the eyes and skin are myelinated first (enabling explorative play essential for further brain development) before the areas that control movement. This means that the other senses are fully developed making it 'safe' for children to take their first steps.

Gustatory (taste)

Contrary to popular belief our tastebuds or receptors are not simply located on the tongue, but also the roof of the mouth and the inside of our cheeks. These are responsible for detecting sweet, salty, sour, bitter and brothy tastes ('umami'), and are greatly enhanced by the sense of smell.

Auditory (hearing)

Our ears are responsible for receiving auditory information but as we shall discover, the inner ear also contains the semi-circular canals responsible for the vestibular system – the sense of gravity and balance. With hearing in the typically developed child near perfect at birth, the ear

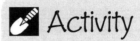 Activity

Cut up different types of food – fruit works well for children to taste. With weaning babies every new food encountered is a sensory adventure, so offer a range of different foods, (one at a time initially) to maximise sensory interest. Older children can try to match tastes to words or pictures. Use common and exotic fruits and offer the whole fruit to feel as well as tasting bite-sized pieces. Talk about the taste, what it is, whether they like it, what it reminds them of, (if anything) and where it grows. All of these will help increase their connections associated with that particular fruit.

is divided into three parts: the inner, middle and outer ear. The external outer ear directs sound waves into the auditory canal from where they travel to the eardrum. A series of vibrations continue to the hammer, anvil and stirrup of the middle ear, which in turn cause another membrane between the middle and inner ear to vibrate along with fluid in the inner ear. This sends electrochemical information through the thalamus to the auditory cortex for further processing. This sound information is processed in the opposite hemisphere of the brain to the ear which received the sound (Olga Bogdashina, 2003).

 ## Activity

Offer a range of resources for spontaneous music-making, e.g. seeds or gravel in homemade shakers, containers covered with fabric to make drums, spoons and saucepans, etc.

Proprioception, kinaesthetic, vestibular

Our lesser-known vestibular, proprioceptive and kinaesthetic senses are responsible for relaying information about gravity and motion (vestibular), muscular movement (kinaesthetic) and our position in space (proprioceptive). Without these vital inner senses, children would not be able to achieve fundamental milestones like taking their first steps, as it is these senses that pass messages to the brain about movement and changes in the position of the head. The vestibular system, which controls balance and movement, is believed to be one of the first of the sensory systems to fully develop, just months after conception. Most of the sensory organs controlling this key role are found in the ears. It is amazing to consider that in little over one year, most children develop from reflex movements at birth to being able to stand, walk and even run. Many of the full-bodied experiences featured in chapter three that require great balance are dependent upon the

development of these inner senses. For most of us our only reminder of the existence of these senses is a bout of travel sickness or feeling dizzy after a spin on a merry-go-round (Carla Hannaford, 1995).

This chapter has introduced some of the different sensory organs and receptors responsible for relaying information to the brain. Although these systems develop largely independently, if we are to live fully functioning lives two key processes are needed:

1. The sensory information needs to be understood; discriminated from other sights, tastes, touch and sounds; stored and accessed; and connected with meaning.

2. The different sources of sensory information need to be integrated to work together to provide us with an accurate representation of the world around us.

It is these connections that are fundamental to learning and memory. More sophisticated and with greater capacity than the most cutting edge computer hard-drive, much of the workings of the brain remain a mystery.

In a world in which our senses are bombarded, you don't have to look far to find sensory-rich play experiences. There are ample opportunities for engaging all the senses through play outdoors, sand and water play, a treasure basket, a collection of heuristic play objects, or other sensory-rich resources. All these activities also offer a multitude of other benefits that make them perfect for supporting the EYFS. Surrounded as we are by resources which have the potential to offer sensory-rich play, choosing where to start and what to focus on in this chapter was quite a challenge! Countless homemade and commercial resources are available to meet this need, but as most settings can access play outdoors, sand, water and a range of household, recycled and natural objects cheaply, freely and easily, it is these resources which will form the basis of our focus. Much of the beauty and appeal of sensory play lies in its flexibility and child-led focus. If we as practitioners use our knowledge of children's interests and our own imagination we can support their play and learning. The following factors are a good starting point in planning sensory-rich provision.

Simplicity

If you've ever commented on how children spend more time playing with the cardboard box than the present it came in, then you will have witnessed some of the appeal and excitement of open-ended resources. When it comes to children's play with toys, generally the simpler the resource, the better. Take the boy aged three to four years whose kitchen role-play never got beyond tipping a basket of play food and plates on the floor. Each time he momentarily paused to look at the toys before walking away. Contrast this with his deep engagement in domestic role play using the objects from a treasure basket. In spontaneous play sessions lasting over an hour (some with sand, others just using the objects on their own) he was observed repeatedly mixing, tossing a chain in a measuring cup ('spaghetti 'perhaps), and wiping up an imaginary spillage with a cloth. Similar child-led play was observed in outdoor play, when he created an

exotic stew of spices, yeast extract, water, soil and plants! This creative play involved searching cupboards for the 'right' ingredients, carefully tipping out spices, scraping gooey yeast extract from a spoon and mixing his fragrant concoction. Judging by the play food alone, it would be easy to assume that domestic role play had little to offer this little boy. But that would miss the point and the potential interest and appeal of open-ended resources as a driver for creativity.

Young children do not have a monopoly on using natural resources and their imagination to conjure up role play. Older children, too, will delight in creating intricate 'fairy meals' using acorn cups for bowls; mixing hearty soups, pies and stews; creating rose petal perfume or lavender

wine; engineering a toxic sludge, a witches potion or cement for construction from mud, sand, twigs, water etc. With access to a few simple household objects like old saucepans, pots, whisks and spoons; some recycled containers; twigs, leaves, seedpods and other natural treasures found outdoors, children's creativity and imagination can have a free reign, provided that children are given the time, space and permission to do so.

Flexibility

Sensory-rich play resources are found all around us and most children do not need any help in signposting these nor instructions on what to do!

As the examples in this chapter illustrate, in the hands of a child, simple yet highly sensory resources can spark creativity and play in children of all ages. This chapter looks at ways of using freely or cheaply available resources to promote sensory play and learning. Sensory play is not an exact science to be slavishly followed. Instead, use these ideas as a springboard for creativity and having fun!

Play with objects

To best support children's play it is helpful to understand some special features of play with objects. As children get older (or more familiar with resources) they move through the process of exploring 'What is this object like?' and 'What can it do?' to 'What can it become?'. These first two phases have been linked to problem solving and the latter to symbolic play. Research has shown that in order to engage in symbolic play younger children need play materials resembling real things to help them represent their play ideas. However, for preschool children and older the reverse is true as open-ended play resources provide greater flexibility for imagination. As we shall see from the **Play snapshots** in this chapter, children's domestic and fantasy role play frequently develops out of their initial investigations (Play England, May 2011).

Play snapshot

In one play session a group of children (aged two to eight years) added biodegradable, loose fill 'peanuts' (similar to polystyrene packing pieces) to water, discovering that when wet it disintegrates to create very realistic effluent scum! Another child spotted the packaging and a small tin and proceeded to see how many pieces he could fit in the tin. He paused several times, explaining that it was full, before devising another strategy to make more space, be it putting the tin lid on to press the pieces down, realising that if he squeezed them with his fingers the pieces got smaller, or putting the tin on the floor so he could press his fingers down with all his weight. Once full, he announced that he wanted to count them to see how many he'd squeezed in and therefore set about emptying the tin. This required another strategy as many of the pieces were now stuck together, so a spoon was needed to prise them out when his finger could no longer reach them. Another child (aged eight) excitedly called out "Look!" as she held up a creation for the other children to see. The subject of excitement and pride was some packaging pieces that she had rolled in sand and couscous to create a look-a-like cheesy nibble! The other children looked on with awe and wonder before sparking a flurry of hands scooping up packaging pieces to use in their own play.

The senses

Picture the average child's toy cupboard and the overriding visual appeal of most toys will probably be apparent. This is often at the expense of stimulating our other senses which, as we discovered in chapter one, are so vital not just for our healthy development but also for our emotional wellbeing. When planning sensory-rich experiences for children, it is important to think about all the senses, rather than just the visual and auditory senses that toys tend to commonly appeal to. This does not mean that each and every experience should be multi-sensory. Indeed, we will discover in chapter four that for some children with sensitivities to sensory stimulation, this can actually be overwhelming. A key part of the adult's role is knowing which sensory stimulation to encourage and support and which to avoid. With careful planning and thought, and only minor changes to provision, the sensory focus of most

play can be fine-tuned. For example, the addition of glitter to sand will change its appearance; washing-up liquid will increase its malleability; dried rice will add textural interest; water will alter its properties; vanilla or peppermint essence will transform its smell; and pea shingle will enhance its sound. Each of these minor changes potentially increases the interest and appeal of sand for children, widening horizons and possibilities and acting as a springboard for further creativity.

 ## Activity

A starting point should be appraising the quality of the existing sensory environment. Spend some time in and outdoors noticing the sensorial qualities of spaces, resources and practices and how these impact upon or contribute to the overall sensory environment.

Children's bodies and brains are typically hard-wired to exploit the full potential of open-ended resources. Sometimes as adults we lose sight of the innate pleasure of simple actions like squelching in squidgy mud, the satisfaction of building a sand castle complete with foaming moat; the challenge of climbing a tree and getting back down safely. For previous generations, sensory play just happened naturally while exploring outdoors and playing with natural and household objects. It is only with increasingly limited access to these experiences, that planned provision becomes necessary. Yet with busy lives we can fail to see beyond the practicalities of mess and dirt to the amazing achievements and creations underway! At the heart of sensory play is giving ourselves time, space and permission to enjoy each resource and in so doing to recapture the essence of what makes experiences like these special and memorable. Where better to start than with adult's most vivid childhood memories of play outdoors, 'running through the wood ... barefoot, making rose petal perfume and making mud pies' (Sue Gascoyne, January 2010).

Outdoor Play

What is it?

Watching a child deeply engrossed in tracing the line of an ant or snail; mesmerised by water slowly dripping into a puddle; delighting in the crunch of frosty blades of grass underfoot; or foraging for seeds for a fairy feast, and the full-bodied absorption and endless play possibilities are apparent. Cobb described 'Nature for the child [as] sheer sensory experience' (1977 quoted in White, 2011, p.70). No matter how small the space, access to an outdoor area offers an ever-changing environment which makes play exciting, varied, unpredictable and challenging. With daily or even hourly changes to light, temperature and weather, as well as the gradual shift from season to season, the outdoors offers a rich and dynamic space. It is this richness, variety and limitlessness that gives resources a high level of 'play affordance' – the ability for children to use resources in different ways, to transform their environment, with endless play possibilities (Gibson, 1979).

The outdoor environment is all about highly sensorial experiences, offering as it does an age and developmentally appropriate backdrop and stimuli for play. Some children may be drawn to creating woodland sculptures, making natural collage pictures and frames and large-scale art. Some may prefer following nature trails, picking a favourite tree, foraging for seed pods, going on minibeast or treasure hunts, digging and planting seeds or investigating with magnifiers. Others will enjoy making mud pies, creating woodland feasts for fairies or witches potions and brews. Experiences which involve the whole of children's bodies are available through climbing trees, creating dens, splashing in mud, making and firing catapults and building obstacle courses. Creativity will come to the fore in making bark rubbings, natural necklaces and mobiles, creating fairy houses and making talking sticks.

The outdoors offers the magic of reading, storytelling, mark-making, and creating music, or simply enjoying a picnic or lying on freshly mown grass watching clouds whizz by. These are just some of the ever-changing possibilities presented by play outdoors.

What you need

As the possibilities for play outdoors are unlimited, the number and type of resources needed will largely be driven by the size of space available; its characteristics, e.g. grass, paving, trees, etc; and the age and interests of the children using the area. Before deciding what to offer and how, it is important to consider:

- How children will access the outdoor environment, e.g. free flow or on a restricted basis?
- How to organise the space and provision so that it offers something different to the indoor space (White, 2011). Being careful not to fill it so much that any benefits of a larger space and scale are lost.
- How to maximise sensory appeal?

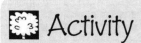 **Activity**

Spend some time outdoors appraising the sensory environment. See how many of your senses are stimulated and think of ways of supporting the lesser-used senses.

A good starting point is watching to see how children naturally play in the outdoor environment and using this to inform planning. Indoor and outdoor provision should be seamlessly linked so that both extend children's learning and are linked to the EYFS. Through careful observations of children's play and listening to them you will discover what, if any, additional resources would best support their play. Consider offering opportunities for all these activities and more by providing:

- Secret den areas for quiet reflection, talking, reading and writing.
- Natural, wild spaces for hiding in, role-play and simply being yourself.
- Messy areas for experimenting with water, sand, mud, etc.
- Areas to actively stimulate the senses.

- Areas for exploring wildlife and natural objects.
- Areas for active play, games and tricycles.
- Storage for children to access and take responsibility for tidying up.

For ideas of specific resources to offer in the outdoor space, see the relevant sections of this chapter together with the many excellent books available focusing on play outdoors.

What to do

- If appropriate, check that the outdoor area is safe and free from urban litter.
- Ensure that children (and adults) are dressed appropriately, whether it be waterproof clothing or sunhats and suncream. Remember that the aim is to prolong play outdoors, not de-sensitise children from the sensory-rich feel of water!
- Watch and listen carefully to better understand and plan for children's play and learning.

Adding extra sensory interest

The ever-changing environment outdoors means that little extra provision should be needed to maximise sensory interest. However, here are a few ideas.

Sight – Add coloured light bulbs or twinkling fairy lights to trees in winter time for the children to enjoy. Hang collections of natural resources, shiny objects and old CDs from tree branches to catch the light and reflect patterns. Hang up camouflage netting for children to see the patterns and shadows created in sunlight. Offer a hose pipe in sunlight for children to recreate the colours of the rainbow in the waterspray. Lay on grass spotting shapes and patterns in clouds.

Sound – Hang objects from branches or a fence to make noises in the breeze. Fill clear plastic containers with gravel, sand, crunchy leaves, acorns, etc. for children to shake and explore as musical instruments. Offer shallow containers of mud, sand, gravel, grass, crisp leaves, etc. for children to squelch and crunch underfoot. Stand or sit outside under umbrellas, a tarpaulin or gazebo to listen to the sound of rain. Splash in lots of puddles to compare the different sounds. Sit in silence listening to the natural sounds that they can hear.

Touch – Close your eyes and go on 'feely walks' in pairs, taking time to feel all the different textures in the garden. Fill bags or shallow containers with crunchy leaves, grass etc. for children to feel in or walk through with eyes open or closed. Create a cosy den in winter for the children to experience the contrasts in temperatures and see their breath.

Smell – Introduce a selection of herbs and 'scented plants' for children to explore and the fragrance to waft on a breeze. Enable children to pick herbs to add to their own special potions. If safe to do so, burn an incense stick or citronella (being careful to avoid dangers from falling ash or wax).

Taste – Plant together salad crops, strawberries and other easy to grow crops for children to enjoy the fruits of their

labour. Pick herbs to add to baking, garnish meals or add to playdough or icy water during play.

Who is this suitable for?

From birth children can access the outdoor environment as a place to lie or sleep in. As well as the health benefits of children accessing lots of fresh air from a young age this appears to be linked to memory, with adults sharing recollections of lying in a pram outdoors, picturing branches swaying or the braided edge of a pram framing their view (Brenda Crowe, 1983, p.10). The decision as to how old children should be before being allowed to explore is matter of personal choice. Rather than imposing specific ages be guided by your own or parents' feelings. Some settings offer the same access to all the babies and children in their care, irrespective of age, but with the young babies do so one-to-one instead. Once children have started crawling they can begin to independently explore the surrounding environment. Play outdoors is particularly great for kinaesthetic learners and boys who benefit greatly from the larger scale and freedom that the outdoors tends to give. As the research mentioned in chapters one and four shows there are great health and wellbeing benefits

of children accessing green space, something that remains with us through to adulthood.

Nature tables

What is it?

Adults of a certain age may recall taking treasured finds into nursery or school for others to share and explore. More often than not these objects may have found their way onto a nature table, with excited 'donors' bristling with pride and onlookers envious or awestruck. Nowadays nature tables generally take two different approaches, each with its own features, purpose and benefits. One approach is to gather a collection of natural objects and display these to promote investigation, exploration, scientific discovery and communication. In contrast, the nature tables found in many Waldorf and Steiner settings tend to take on greater 'spiritual' significance. Reflecting the changing seasons, these are often themed to include make-believe figures, natural features and a colour coordinated cloth backdrop. Primarily used to inspire discussion, imagination and role-play, this more spiritually-rooted approach helps nurture an awareness of the changing seasons and a respect for

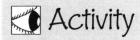 Activity

Talk in your team about what objects, if any, they can recall taking in to school or nursery and how it made them feel? Were they allowed to touch the objects? How did this make them feel? What did they think or feel about the nature table? Was it boring; something to excitedly check to see what was new; something that made them feel proud or excluded as their items were never picked to be displayed?

In many settings and schools 'Show and Tell' seems to have taken on a different meaning, with children taking in new (invariably plastic or licensed) toys and other 'trophies' rather than nature finds. If this applies to children in your setting talk about how you could introduce a weekly or monthly nature focus, with children invited to bring in objects or pictures of things that they have found and would like to share. How could you ensure a balance between keeping the objects 'safe' and allowing children to be engaged? How could you use the nature table as an active part of planning and provision? Compare sessions with nature finds and those with toys. Talk with the children about which sessions they most enjoyed and why. Explore whether any changes could improve the experience still further.

 Activity

Invite a group of practitioners to each bring in a special or unusual natural object to share. Each person draws two columns on a piece of A4 paper (vertical), writing what their object is and why they like it at the top of each column. Fold over the top so that it can't be read and arrange on a table next to the object. Practitioners spend time looking at and exploring the objects in silence. When appropriate, they can record on the relevant piece of paper what they think that object is and what, if anything, they like about it. Practitioners should fold over to conceal their writing, creating a concertina fold, before exploring the next item and recording their thoughts on the relevant piece of paper. After plenty of time sit in a circle on the floor to explore together the objects one at a time. The person who selected each object can read out the suggested 'answers' from the sheet of paper before revealing what it actually is. Talk about any surprises, things they have discovered and what resources, if any, they could offer to further extend children's learning and exploration. Try putting ideas into practice with children and seeing how they respond to a new nature 'table'.

the beauty of nature all around us. There is of course scope for overlap between the two, with an open and hands-on approach which encourages children to use natural objects as props for role-play and storytelling or to inspire exploration and discovery.

Some parallels can be drawn between the carefully selected treasures in a treasure basket and the objects picked for a nature table like a fossil, feather, birds egg/nest, shell or seedpod. Each item has been picked for its specialness, differentness or 'wow' factor. Research into the benefits of nature tables by Tomkins and Tunnicliffe has revealed that young children (and to a lesser extent older children) are drawn to an object's colour, shape, texture, feel, weight, size and beauty. The sensory dimension and aesthetic appeal of objects was apparent. For example, the look, feel and beauty of a fossil, feather, pebble, red berries and jewel-like salt crystals were particularly appealing to five- and six-year-olds and provided a great springboard for further exploration and animated discussion. If used proactively to engage children, a nature table was felt to have a 'positive effect

upon [children's] attitude, and development of knowledge and language and communication skills' (Stephen Tomkins and Sue Tunnicliffe, 2007).

The attitude of the adult offering the nature table will determine the degree to which children feel able to actively engage with the objects in hands-on exploration and play, and the risk that the nature table becomes a static display for children to simply 'look at but don't touch'.

Adding extra sensory interest

Sight – Try turning off the main lights and just shining a lamp, torch or safety candle on the table. Use coloured light bulbs or twinkling fairy lights to create a sense of awe and wonder. Look at the objects through a transparent plastic sheet, with sunglasses, colour paddles or magnifying glasses. Add mirrors to the display to help children see the objects from different perspectives. Incorporate an overhead projector to provide another view of the objects.

Sound – Use sound tapes to accompany the objects being observed. This can help set the scene or focus on a particular theme. Offer some non-fragile exhibits in clear plastic bottles or shoe boxes for the children to shake and explore.

Touch – Lay bubble wrap or another material over the table for the children to touch the objects through. Experiment with eyes open and closed. Can they guess what the objects are?

Smell – A scented candle or incense stick could be used to create a calming environment. Try simply smelling the artefacts, as many of these are likely to have their own pungent smells! Fresh lavender, cut grass or flower petals could add extra olfactory appeal. Put some of the artefacts in lidded containers to emphasise their smell.

Taste – If using nature tables with very young children you will need to carefully select objects that are safe to be mouthed. Alternatively, offer opportunities for experiencing the objects whilst sat in very small groups, each feeling and smelling the different objects with adult supervision.

Who is this suitable for?

As a table of objects this is most suited to children aged three to four years through to eleven years of age for free exploration. However with supervision, specific objects can be offered to babies and toddlers in one-to-one explorations or small groups. Like the objects in a treasure basket, these should be selected for their special qualities and appeal, and have regard to safety.

Mud Play

What is it?

"Young children have a deep affinity and fascination with the earth and its natural materials. Such play engages children and gives practitioners motivating contexts and themes for supporting their learning. Children will spend long periods of time lost in their own worlds as they explore the feel and behaviour of the materials or play out imaginary scenes and stories to themselves". (Judith Stevens, 2006, p.20).

Mud is an example of a malleable material, which like clay, playdough, pastry and plasticine can be moulded into a range of shapes by even very young children without needing tools or specialist equipment. Like sand, mud has its own unique properties and 'behaviours' which with time and ample experimentation, children will come

to understand and master. Unlike some other malleable resources, mud is freely available and has the potential to create vivid and lasting memories, as adults' recollections of making mud pies testify.

What you need

Just as with water play most children don't need any specific provision in order to engage with mud. Rather they need the time, space and 'permission' to do so! Before deciding which resources to provide to enhance muddy play, spend some time watching children playing during or immediately after a downpour. What do they do? What evidence, if any, is there of what they might be thinking? Do they use the mud in unexpected ways? Notice any language and communication and reflect with the children on their likes and dislikes before planning to meet their needs.

As a minimum you will need:

- An area of top soil (free from urban litter) e.g. a builders tray, 'grow bag' or even a window box.
- Suitable clothing for very messy play.

Beyond this, the following possible resources are all optional:

- A range of garden tools or implements for digging, exploration or role play.
- A selection of containers for transporting, mixing up potions, using to make mud castles including: buckets, watering cans, sieves, spoons and wheel barrows.
- Collections of natural objects, e.g. conkers, leaves, twigs, pine cones, etc. (preferably collected by the children as this will have far greater relevance and appeal).
- Collections of household objects, e.g. old spoons, whisks, measuring pots, sink plugs etc.
- Collections of mark-making resources, e.g. rollers, paint brushes, twigs, spatulas, plant mister sprays.
- Collections of rubber and plastic mini-beasts, small-world characters or vehicles.

Activity

Take some time to explore mud yourself. First experiment with clean dry soil: explore it with your fingers and focus on what it feels like. (You can put the soil in a tray or other container indoors or better still play outdoors.) Next, pick one or two natural objects to play with in the soil. These could be stones, leaves or twigs, some spoons or a (washable) item from a treasure basket. Explore the resources doing whatever feels right, whether this be making patterns, building mounds, mark-making (with a finger or stick) etc. Add water if wished to continue your exploration, sculpture, building, role-play, pattern-making and mark-making. Follow your instinct about how to use the soil/mud, e.g. with objects, your hands, bare feet or wellington boots for stamping in. If using objects, what would you choose and how would you use them, e.g. recycled yoghurt pots for transporting, making mud pies, construction, etc. If possible repeat this activity outdoors or with a group of adults or children to see how it compares.

TIP: If you really don't like putting your hands in soil then use a spoon or stick instead and see if you are gradually able to do so. If possible try playing on your own first, as this will provide a contrast to the experience of playing alongside other adults or children.

Reflection: Spend a few minutes thinking about:

- What you most enjoyed.
- What you least enjoyed, e.g. getting messy.
- What, if anything, surprised you?
- What you would like to do differently or more of?
- Did you find any difference between how you played and felt when playing indoors or outside?
- Did you find a difference between your play on your own and play with other people?
- What, if any, fresh perspective has this given to your play with soil and mud?
- Will you change anything about what you offer children (e.g. time, resources, space)?
- Is there anything that you would change about your role?
- How could you make mud play more accessible to children who don't enjoy getting messy?

What to do

If necessary, first carry out a risk assessment on the area to ensure children's health and safety is protected. Then simply observe children's free play, without providing any special resources, to see if and how they are already accessing muddy play. Play with mud and soil offers lots of opportunities for digging, planting seeds, splashing in muddy puddles, making welly prints and exploring the different muddy tracks made by toy and real vehicles. Children can use mud to create a wormery, make compost, engage in mud fights, create sculptures, inspire role play or small-world play.

Observe and note how children are playing, whether it is appealing to children of different ages and any differences in how boys and girls play? Consider what if anything you can do to further extend play, being careful not to destroy the naturalness or spontaneity in the process. Be sure to offer access at different times, e.g. after a downpour, so children can see the natural effects of nature.

Play snapshot

In one observation of a two- and six-year-old on a winter's day, the pair energetically worked together digging soil to fill a wheelbarrow with mud. They then found a source of water to add to the soil to create a muddy concoction. Next, sprigs of foliage and twigs were added, each child taking it in turn to stir the heavy mixture. With the mix ready, the six year old scooped handfuls out onto the grass, moulding this into a carefully rounded mound with both hands. The two-year-old meanwhile continued mixing and perfecting the barrow full of 'horse feed' for his imaginary horse 'William'.

Numerous aspects of the curriculum can be seen in this snapshot, from the cooperative working, focus and concentration; creativity and imagination; gross and fine motor skills; and problem solving and scientific discovery. It also shows how easily adults can misinterpret play, as the observer assumed the children were making mud pies, not horse feed!

 Adding extra sensory interest

Sight – Add glitter, sequins or shells. Drizzle (non-toxic) paint into the mud and experiment with mixing. Explore whether florescent and glittery paints remain visible. Does the coloured paint disappear or the mud change colour? Use sticks and natural objects to experiment with mark-making.

Sound – Add lentils, pea shingle, dried rice, smooth glass pebbles, gravel or shells to mud to increase the sound potential. Add water to the mud and experiment with movement to alter the sound quality.

Touch – Play with hands and bare fee. Add dried pasta or rice, shells or stones for extra texture or to improve building qualities. Feathers or seeds can add great textural interest. Autumn leaves will give initial 'crunch' to the texture before turning to soggy slime. If children are reluctant to touch mud, offer sticks and other utensils or tools to enable them to join in.

Smell – Add essential oils such as lavender or eucalyptus for extra olfactory appeal. Add spices or fresh herbs – mint, cinnamon or star anise, all have very distinctive smells.

Taste – Some children's play will naturally turn to making concoctions and meals without ever considering tasting it! One adult reflected upon how when she was young she'd mixed tomato ketchup with mud pies to make delicious treats to sell. She described the pungent smell of tomato and mud and how no-one had bought any of her creations! Some children may be drawn to tasting the mud, and opinion is divided over whether this should be discouraged or whether in fact this is good for developing a healthy immune system. Obviously, eating soil and mud should not be actively encouraged. If appropriate, consider recreating meals of 'worms' (wholemeal spaghetti) and 'mud pies' (mashed potato and gravy), muddy stones (meatballs) or creating 'gravel or stones' (from flapjack held together with sultana or date 'mud').

Who is this suitable for?

Always carry out a risk assessment on the area first to ensure children's health and safety. Talk to children about the importance of them washing their hands with soap after play and not touching their eyes or mouth. Soil can contain harmful bacteria so, if offering to babies, do so on a one-to-one basis. If offering to young children do so in small groups. Babies can be supported in their investigations by holding them as they 'stand' on soil, or by sprinkling it on their fingers or toes. Whatever age you choose to offer it to, it is important that you yourself are comfortable so that children do not pick up any concerns. If appropriate, babies and young children can play with gloop, tapioca or clean sand instead.

Sand Play

What is it?

Few children could resist an opportunity to play with sand. Like water play, the flexibility of sand gives it almost magical qualities. Matterson comments on the special qualities of sand which need to be experienced first to be understood (1975). Dry sand is great for pouring and filling. It can feel cold or warm to touch, squeaks when squashed and moves in an intriguing way, behaving more like a liquid than a solid. When water is added to sand its properties and texture are, bit by bit, transformed opening up the potential for mark-making, pattern-making, imprints, shapes, construction and manipulation. Add 'too much' water and it changes again to a sloppy liquid, great for

pouring and filling; wonderfully responsive to stamping and sploshing, and creating 'slurping' sound effects. Allow the watery sand to settle and the sand and water separate or the water dries up, reversing the whole process. Given this wealth of possibilities, it is easy to see children's special fascination for sand.

Whether offered a beach, a deep purpose-built sand tray, or a makeshift container of sand, children will find much to occupy and excite them. With the simple addition of water, some containers for digging and transporting, or some smooth pebbles or unusual shells, play can be further extended and transformed. In the hands of a resourceful individual, sand on its own has the potential to be a lunar landscape, a desert scene, a blank canvass, a truly interactive 'whiteboard', an exotic meal, a witches'

brew, fairy potion or simply enjoyed for its exciting or calming properties. I recently took a few minutes to explore sand and a selection of beautiful natural objects and was amazed at the feel of the fine sand particles sifting between my fingers; surprised by the solid feel of a handful of sand in my clenched fist and how this slowly then quickly changed as the sand finally worked its way free leaving my hand empty; delighted at the patterns created first with my fingers and later using natural objects; and the dune-like ridges left on my outstretched fingers as the sand fell away. The experience was deeply satisfying, all-absorbing and calm and I understood in an instant just how frustrating it must be as a child to be interrupted for tea or clearing up!

What you will need

- Play sand or silver sand.
- Shallow and deep tray/bowl/container.

You can also offer nearby one or more of the following collections of resources:

- Collection of objects – spoons, brushes, sieves, containers – e.g. measuring pots, mini-flowerpots, etc.
- Collection of small-world figures, vehicles or animals, mini-beasts, etc.
- Recycled containers and objects – e.g. clean yoghurt and cream pots, cream and margarine tubs, plastic fruit punnets, etc.
- Collections of natural objects – e.g. twigs, pine cones, leaves, seed pods, etc.
- Collections of investigative resources – e.g. magnifiers, mirrors, diffracters, magnets, colour paddles, etc.
- Water – Ideally in a jug which children can pour, with more water available from an outside tap.
- A hose pipe, guttering and containers for transporting water.

Arrange the collections so that they are accessible but not in the sand, so that children can choose whether to combine the resources or not. Offer inside or preferably outdoors.

 # Activity

Take some time to explore sand yourself, ideally on your own without children. First experiment with dry sand, scooping up handfuls and feeling it fall between your fingers. Try to see how many different things you can do with the sand and focus on what it feels like and the sound that it makes when squeezed. Next pick one or two natural objects to play with in the sand. This could be a special stone, shell or twig or an item from a treasure basket. Explore the resources doing whatever feels right, whether this be making patterns, burying the object or rolling it across the sand. Enjoy the calming feel of the sand and notice your patterns of thought. After ample time (or on another occasion) you could try adding some water to the sand to explore. Do so gradually to experiment with what you can do with the sand and how the consistency changes. Follow your instinct about how to use the wet sand and what objects to use, if any. If possible repeat this activity outdoors or with a group of adults or some children to see how it compares.

TIP: Avoid using plastic sand tools as this a chance to see what happens when you use objects that you wouldn't expect to find in sand. (If you really don't like putting your hands in sand then start with an object instead and see if you are gradually able to do so.) Notice the calming effects of playing quietly alone.

Reflection: Spend a few minutes thinking about:

- What did you most enjoy?
- What, if anything, surprised you?
- What would you like to do differently or again?
- Did you find any difference between how you played and how you felt when playing indoors or outside?
- Did you find a difference to your play when alone compared to play with other people?
- What, if any, fresh perspective has this given to play with sand?
- Is there anything you will change about what you offer children (e.g. time, resources, space, containers for resource)?
- Is there anything that you would change about your role?

What to do

Observe

Simply sit nearby and observe the children's play noting what each child is doing, how they are playing with the sand and which of the resources they are using and how. Record any language spoken, notable changes in play or communication, and which particular aspects of sand play or exploration appear to be offering greatest interest and appeal. Listen to the children's communication with each other and watch body language, sustained shared thinking and deep focus. Note any play themes that emerge, e.g. super heroes, mummies and daddies, a trip to the hospital. This will help you to better support and extend play if needed by the provision of more time, space, materials or support.

Support

If appropriate:

- Play alongside the children being careful not to dominate or change the focus of play.
- Model using appropriate vocabulary for tools, processes and outcomes. Using correct words like rake, trowel and sow is much better for supporting children's thinking, learning and independence.
- Introduce relevant open-ended questions to support and extend thinking. You will need to tune into children's play and be sensitive to avoid disrupting or redirecting play.
- Re-group any unused collections of resources during play, being careful not to give children the impression that you are hurrying them or tidying up.

Plan

Use your individual and team observations of what resources, type of play and language they used as a basis for planning for children's needs and interests in relation to the EYFS.

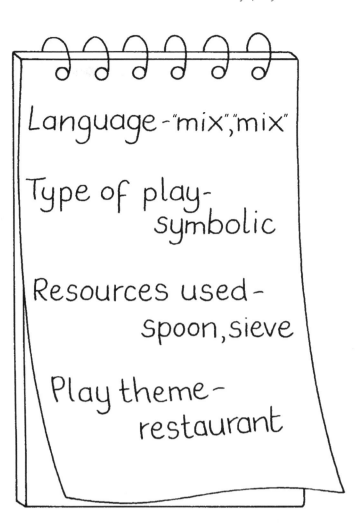

Language - "mix","mix"

Type of play - symbolic

Resources used - Spoon, sieve

Play theme - restaurant

👶 Activity

Here's an experiment to try. Put some sand in two bowls in different areas of the outdoor space. Add some plastic sand tools, (e.g. a spade, rake, mini bucket) next to one bowl of sand to see what children do. Offer some objects found in a treasure basket, heuristic play resources or natural items next to the other bowl. Observe play carefully to see how children use the sand and resources, e.g. explorative, play, pretend play and any noteworthy language or other responses. Record the length of time that they play at each sand area.

Repeat with children of different ages, at different times, offering only one type of sand provision at a time. Adapt to follow children's lead, e.g. position near an outside tap and containers, sieves, funnels etc to see how this changes play. Reflect upon how the children played, any differences or surprises. Do our findings have any implications for future provision?

 Adding extra sensory interest

Sight – Add glitter, sequins, glass pebbles, shells, multi-coloured beads or finger paint to wet or dry sand. Line the base of the container with tin foil or a safety mirror to provide surprise and extra interest. Offer different coloured sand, either picked to support a play theme, or a contrasting colour. Stand a mirror up vertically to divide the tray in half and use for mark-making and pattern-making.

Sound – Add dried lentils, pea shingle, dried rice, glass pebbles or shells to add extra sounds.

Touch – Offer in a range of containers, i.e. shallow, deep, transparent, to see the effects upon play. Add washing-up liquid to change the malleability of the sand. Add beads; dried rice, couscous or lentils; or pea shingle to add textural interest. Bury treasure-like objects, e.g. a chain, pots etc, in the sand for an archaeological dig. Add salt and dried lentils or rice to sand and explore capacity as well as what happens when the children try to sift it.

Smell – Add vanilla or peppermint essence, fruit tealeaves, fresh mint or rosemary leaves to add sensory interest. Consider the smells of wet and dry sand.

Taste – Most children will try to taste sand at least once, but it is obviously not something to be actively encouraged! Others will be content simply with creating imaginary meals, or making picnic food to eat on a pretend trip to the seaside.

Who this is suitable for?

If sand is clean and play with very young children is closely supervised, there is no reason to deny this richly sensory play to even very young babies in a shallow tray of sand. Offer long-handled objects, twigs and containers for children who struggle to touch sand ('tactile defensive') to use instead. With babies and young children if you do need an alternative, try dried rice flakes, couscous, polenta or sugar instead of sand.

Water Play

What is it?

Like sand, water provides countless opportunities for exploration and play and similar scope for harnessing its special qualities. A bowl of water offers great noise-making potential, from the sound of fat droplets of water, noisy splashes, gentle lapping, the delicate 'thin' sound of water corkscrewing from a funnel, or satisfyingly 'fat' sound of pouring from a jug or container. With the addition of bubbles or colour sensory appeal is increased. Use warm water or add ice cubes for a different sensory feel. Freeze blocks of ice or thin glass-like sheets for a whole myriad of different experiences. Explore the effects of water and light on refraction and its magnifying properties. Discover the power of water to transport, support weight, shape channels and landscapes or change other materials like sand and soil. Experience rain and its sound and feel; the magic of snow; and experiment with the effects of salt on ice. Make lollies or drinks; explore the trajectory from hose pipes; or the 'coriolis effect' as water swirls down a plug hole. Inspire domestic role-play or small-world play. The versatility of water offers endless potential to be moulded and

for 'water painting' and mark-making. If painting with water infused with lemon juice, children can create their own secret messages on paper. (They will need to heat up the ink for it to show so can experiment with different ways of achieving this.)

Touch – Add washing-up liquid to change the feel of water. Add beads, dried rice, dried couscous, lentils or pea shingle to add textural interest and explore sinking or floating. Vary with warm and ice cold water. Add ice cubes for role-play and to increase the sensory experience or blocks of ice to the water tray to replicate icebergs. (Use gloves).

Smell – Add vanilla or peppermint essence, essential oils, fruit tealeaves, fresh mint leaves or bubble bath (check allergies first). Squeeze fresh lemon into the water or infuse hot water with lavender, rosemary, lemon or orange peel before cooling and introducing play; allow children to mix potions and experiment with different mixtures of smells.

Sound – Add dried lentils, rice and pasta, sand, pea shingle, glass pebbles or shells to containers for pouring and stirring. Offer metal or wooden kitchen implements such as spoons, tea strainers and whisks to explore sound potential.

Taste – Many children will enjoy trying the water, but as it is being used for play this is not something to actively encourage. Invite experimentation through making drinks or lollies instead.

Who is this suitable for?

Most children across the ages enjoy playing with water. With babies make water play (or bath time) fun by adding or blowing bubbles with a straw, introducing songs and rhymes, tickling and peek a boo games. With very young babies do so on a one-to-one basis. Most toddlers love washing up or bathing baby dolls, so support this where possible. Not only will they be replicating some of what they may see at home but they will also enjoy a sensory-rich experience and be learning through experimentation.

Have a tea party outside with lots of opportunities for children to pour, fill, get wet and be creative. Supervise children at all times. Never leave children unattended with water, no matter how shallow the water is.

Treasure Baskets, Heuristic and 'Loose Parts' Play
What is it?

A treasure basket is a sturdy natural basket brimming full of 'treasures' picked for their variety, sensory appeal and interest. First developed in the 1940s for babies aged seven to twelve months, treasure baskets stem from Elinor Goldschmied's observations of children's fascination for playing with commonly available household objects. In recent years there has been a growing recognition of the value of this type of sensory-rich resource for older children too. As well as natural items treasure baskets should include objects made from metal, stone, cardboard, wood, fabric, rubber and leather, and be of a size and scale suitable for child-size hands. To maximise interest select objects with a mix of colours, functions and shapes. The

treasures should move in different ways, have different weights, textures and properties and collectively appeal to all the senses. The aim is to create a collection of beautiful objects, each selected for their own merits. I have seen treasure baskets of interesting and sensory-rich objects 'devalued' by the addition of a large empty cardboard tissue box, a coat hanger and large pieces of bubble wrap or fabric, simply added to fill the basket. Far better to include less objects initially, each with their own intrinsic quality and appeal, than add inferior quality objects that will give the resource the appearance of a waste receptacle.

Babies and young children's brains are hard wired to search for novelty and pattern (John Brierely, 1994) so a carefully sourced treasure basket provides literally a world in a basket. The unique qualities of each individual item help make this resource special. But their juxtaposition with objects that you would not expect to find next to each other adds to this, promoting endless opportunities for problem solving and creativity. Even very young babies sit happily absorbed in play for an hour or more. It instinctively appeals to their senses without needing adult involvement. Recent practitioner-led research explored what happened when two mats were laid on the floor in a room, one with conventional plastic toys, the other with treasure basket objects on it. Over a number of sessions the practitioners observed which resources the children chose to play with. The results were resounding, with all the children selecting the open-ended treasure basket objects in preference to traditional toys.

Like many adults reflecting upon their vivid childhood play memories (Sue Gascoyne, 2010), you may recall playing with pots and pans or Granny's button box and the endless play potential that these simple objects offered. Children naturally see the world differently to adults, so for a child a wooden block can become a phone, mini-house, spoon and more. Young children have a well-observed fascination with these everyday household objects that can be difficult for us adults to understand. If you need a reminder try the activity overleaf.

What you need

A treasure basket is just that, a basket full of treasure-like objects. You will need:

- A sturdy round wicker or natural basket measuring 10" to 14" in diameter and 4" to 5" deep. If struggling to source the right basket, the most important features are its sturdiness and depth – it should be deep enough for children to have to dig through to find objects and experience a sense of discovering 'real treasure'.
- 30 to 80 natural and household objects, picked for their sensory appeal, quality, play potential and 'wow factor'. These should be child-size in scale and each contribute something to the overall sensory experience. Avoiding actual toys and plastic makes the resource all the more special.
- Consider zoning the play space with a cosy floor mat. This can increase concentration and focus, improving learning outcomes.

What to do

The adult's role is essential in providing a well-maintained, stimulating resource and the space and time for its

Activity

Sit with a bag of natural and household objects or an actual treasure basket and take the time to feel the objects, with your eyes closed. People tend to find an object that intrigues them and can't help but to find out what it is! If this applies to you, try to resist peeping and simply put the object to one side so that you can look at it when finished. Once you've fully explored the objects by feel alone (using hands and feet), look at the basket or selection of objects and see which of them you find most appealing. (Note whether these objects are the same ones which you enjoyed feeling.) If looking at the objects try putting the collection in an attractive basket to see if and how it changes the appeal of the objects.

Now repeat with a selection of conventional toys. Which set of resources did you prefer the feel of? Which did you find more interesting? Did the process trigger any memories?

TIP: Try playing outdoors instead. If possible try on your own first, as this will provide a contrast to playing alongside other adults or children.

Reflection: Spend a few minutes thinking about:

- What you most enjoyed playing with and how?
- What, if anything surprised you?
- What you would like to do differently or explore more of again another time?
- Did you find any difference between how you played and how you felt when playing indoors/ outside, alone/with others?
- Has this changed your view of play with a treasure basket?
- Is there anything you would change about what you offer children? E.g. time for play, contents of the basket, the mat that the basket is offered on (to create a treasure basket 'zone' and increase focus), space, frequency, time of day offered, length of time offered for, where the resource is offered, accessibility of basket, age of children offered the resource, etc.?
- Is there anything that you would change about your role, e.g. less hands-on, more supportive, more enlightened observations?

exploration. But babies and children generally need no explanation or introduction to help them get the most from a treasure basket. Clear the room or outdoor space of resources and ensure that the baby or child is sat safely on the floor, supported by cushions if needed. Position the basket next to or in front of the child, or group of children, and sit back and enjoy observing their play. Try not to ask questions, offer particular objects or comment on play. Instead, let the children show you what they are interested in. Some adults may struggle to take a 'back seat' but cast your mind back to a moment when you were happily engrossed in something, it could be a favourite TV programme, a great book or a game. How did you feel when you were interrupted and abruptly pulled out of your own little world?

Although originally intended for babies, play with a treasure basket seems to offer older children something valuable and special too. Treasure baskets offer important creative and age-appropriate opportunities to older children because they also benefit from:

- Richly sensory objects that make up a treasure basket;
- The inclusion of often 'forbidden objects', such as pottery and glass;
- The juxtaposition of highly contrasting objects, textures, materials, and properties.

Watching young and old children absorbed in play with a treasure basket is a magical experience and gives a fantastic insight not just into children's interests, developmental levels and schemas, but also their world.

Using the 'Sensory Play Continuum' of stages (Sue Gascoyne, 2009, see page 36) as a tool for further expanding the play potential of treasure baskets, can help children get the most from these amazing resources. It also helps provide adults with a steer on the thorny issue of when and how best to support play. The three stages of play are loosely based upon actual observations of play with a treasure basket and can help us get the right balance between adult and child-initiated play as recommended in the EPPE report (Iram Siraj-Blatchford et al., 2004).

Stage 1 – Free play

Babies and children play freely with the resources without any adult involvement. (Although adult supervision is needed.)

Stage 2 – Combining resources

The treasure basket is offered next to another resource such as sand, water, magnets or mirrors, to further extend its appeal and play potential. This, the second stage of the Continuum (Sue Gascoyne, 2009) was found to be the most highly creative stage of play in research observations (Sue Gascoyne, 2010). Children love to pour, transport, make patterns and engage in role-play, so by combining these with objects from the basket the level of 'play affordance' or potential (Gibson, 1979) significantly increases.

- Try offering a treasure basket next to water, sand, dried couscous, rice, mirrors or magnets. Children typically

love combining resources so be prepared for some deeply focussed or highly imaginative play!
- Choose whether to offer the whole basket of objects for a child to pick from or a selection which will not be ruined.
- Offer the basket outside and you won't need to worry about any mess!
- Always check allergies first.

Stage 3 – Adult-initiated play

The final stage of the Continuum involves using simple adult-initiated activities with a treasure basket. Many may be inspired by children themselves.

- Weighing activities – picking two objects and children pretending that their arms are an old-fashioned set of balancing scales to try to work out which object is heavier - great for problem solving.
- Threading – onto ribbon or string to explore holes – this will particularly appeal to children with a trajectory schema and is great for hand-eye coordination and fine motor skills.
- Sink or swim – guessing which objects will sink and which will float in water – great for problem solving and developing thinking skills.
- Buried treasure – when treasure-like objects are buried in sand and children use brushes and spoons in a mini-archaeological dig. Later magnets can be added for a foray into metal detecting – great for fine motor skills and imagination.

In this third stage, the adult's role is more proactive, picking activities based on children's interests and abilities and supporting or extending children's questions, discovery and thinking. Through support and facilitation, the adult's skill and sensitivity, and crucially from building upon children's interests and developmental levels, children can be helped to move to the Zone of Proximal Development, where learning is extended beyond what they would achieve through independent play. (Lev Vygotsky, 1978.)

Adding extra sensory interest

Sight – Ensure objects are of varying colours to add visual interest. Select objects with a range of different features and characteristics, e.g. plain, patterned, shiny, dull, big, small, clear, opaque, etc.

Sound – Offer objects with a range of different properties to maximise the potential for exploring noise-making. Metal will make a very different sound to wood. Provide a number of containers and objects that can be used for filling and emptying. Containers that can be filled with other objects make great shakers. Containers that can be beaten with hands, or long-handled objects to make beaters, create great drums. Research revealed children's apparent preference for playing with metal objects. Could this be in part because of its noise-making qualities?

Touch – Provide materials with different properties e.g. metal, wood, fabric, cardboard, rubber, stone, shell, wicker, pottery, glass etc. This will provide a sensory smorgasbord of textures and properties like smooth/rough, warm/cold, heavy/light, soft/hard, prickly, etc. Use bags, boxes and blankets to cover and hide the objects. Explore with your hands or feet. Experiment with eyes open and then closed.

Smell – Create added olfactory interest through the inclusion of metal, leather and rubber items, each with their own distinct smell. A lavender bag or mini-fabric bags filled with rosemary or thyme subtly introduces smell to a treasure basket. Infuse cotton pads with perfumed oil or add spices like cinnamon sticks and cloves or herbs, to mini-bags. (Check allergies first and ensure that bags are securely sewn or tied shut). Add a fresh orange, lemon or lime, pricked first with a fork, as a temporary addition. (Be sure to check regularly and remove before it goes mouldy.) Older children can try smelling different objects with their eyes shut. If you focus enough most objects such as rubber, leather, metal or wood have their own distinct smell.

Taste – Many children will instinctively mouth the treasure basket items as this is a natural phase in exploration. For this reason, items should be chosen that are safe to be mouthed, regularly checked and cleaned with soapy water or replaced when needed. Avoid treasure basket play when children have streaming colds to minimise the chance of cross contamination. Alternatively select objects that can be washed and allow each child to explore their own set of objects, with supervision of course. Older children too may be seen mouthing unfamiliar objects to try to understand what they are. This is a perfectly natural step in exploration, problem solving and discovery.

Who is this suitable for?

Although children aged six months to six years are likely to get the most from this type of play, some of the objects found within a treasure basket have even been given to premature babies to provide much needed sensory

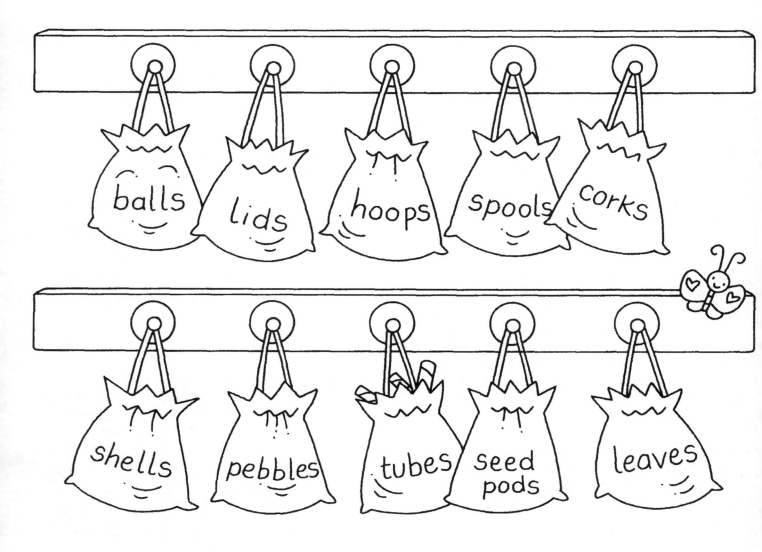

stimulation. Obviously select the objects with care and supervise at all times. At the opposite end of the spectrum, adults with learning difficulties and even the elderly are enjoying the special appeal of play with a treasure basket, so there really are no limits to play.

Play with objects

What is it?

Heuristic play, meaning 'discovery play' was the term coined by Elinor Goldschmied and Anita Hughes for play by one to two year olds with lots of different objects. Heuristic play involves collecting lots of bags (about 20 or more) each containing a similar type of object, e.g. one for curtain hoops, another for jam jar lids, and others for corks, table

tennis balls, etc. The adult clears the room of other toys and attractively arranges the mini-collections of resources on the floor. Several large tins and other containers are added for children to use for sorting. Children play uninterrupted, exploring the almost limitless permutations for playing with the resources. This type of play is considered to be perfect for this age as children can incorporate their newly developed mobility and are not expected to share! The adult's role is to:

- Subtly rearrange the collections during play to give 'clarity' to the resources, for example by re-grouping similar objects;
- Observe children's play, noticing what they play with and how, and whether their play is solitary or with others;
- Orchestrate tidying up the objects and involving all the children in sorting the different objects into their

separate bags with simple and clear instructions, like "Who can find a ball like this?".

- Check the objects as they are tidied away to make sure that they are in good order.

 ## Activity

Either select two or three existing bags of heuristic play items or gather together some objects to start a collection. Try hoops, lids and ball sets for starters. Spend some time exploring the objects quietly. Experiment with using the objects in different ways. How many different ways can you come up with for using the objects? Play in a group instead and compare findings. What else do you need to extend your play, e.g. large tins for collecting and sorting, a mug tree, a kitchen towel holder, different types of objects in other bags? Observe a session with children playing quietly. What sorts of benefits, schemas (repeated patterns of behaviour like transporting, enveloping, lining up), examples of experimentation, trial and error, problem solving, sorting, etc can you spot?

Reflection: Spend a few minutes thinking about...

- How does the children's play and concentration compare with their play and focus on other things? Reflect as a team on how best you can improve heuristic play provision for children, e.g. offer more frequently, change or add to the resources, reconsider the area in which they are offered, allow more time, etc.

'Loose parts' are materials (such as tyres, crates, pallets, tubing) that can be moved, combined, re-designed, lined up, taken apart and put back together in any number of ways. Like heuristic play objects, they have no specific set of directions and can be used alone or combined with other materials. Their aim is to stimulate, facilitate and enhance children's play. Depending upon the objects selected, they are suitable for three- to four-year-olds up to and including secondary school children.

Loose parts resources should be checked first for any obvious safety risks. The aim is to manage the level of risk to an acceptable level, rather than designing out all challenge. Loose parts play encourages children to conduct their own risk assessments. The premise is that if we take away all risk, children will never learn how to judge situations for themselves. Observations have shown that if children are not presented with challenging enough resources, they will adapt their play to increase the risk and challenge. An obvious example of this is children climbing up a slide or coming down head first, rather than sliding down on their bottom!

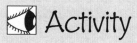

Activity

Gather a selection of recycled resources, e.g. plastic bakers trays, car tyres, fabric, cardboard tubing, guttering, carpet off cuts and pallets outdoors for you to experiment with. Explore in a group. Compare playing freely and experimenting with the scrap. Challenge yourselves to create something specific such as a mode of transport, or to solve a problem, for example getting to the other side of the playground without touching the floor, or to come up with the most amount of different uses and ideas for the material.

Reflection: Spend a few minutes thinking about:

- Any discoveries, surprises, likes and dislikes?
- What implications, if any does this have upon existing play provision?

Unlike treasure baskets, whose primary focus is sensory exploration (and the problem and solving and creativity that this sparks), heuristic play offers collections of similar objects, selected more for their easy access and play potential than sensory appeal. The resulting play may actually look very similar, with older children exploring cause and effect, trial and error, construction, sorting, patterns and problem solving as well as pretend play. When older children play with a treasure basket, many aspects of their experimentation could be described as heuristic play. The key factor in common is their open-ended play potential and fact that there are no right or wrong ways of playing. This is true of both the treasures in a treasure basket and the objects in a heuristic play collection. Similarly 'loose parts' play is characterised by open-ended play with different objects and materials, albeit on a larger scale. So the plug or wooden spoon of a treasure basket; or curtain rings, corks and tins of heuristic play are replaced by car tyres, cardboard tubes and crates of 'loose parts' play. Loose parts play involves full-bodied experiences and is great for problem solving, encouraging cooperative working, firing imagination and creativity, increasing physical development and supporting personal, social and emotional development.

Other sensory play resources

As well as the staple sensory resources identified, countless homemade and commercial resources are also available. Many people associate sensory play with messy food play,

but as this chapter has shown this would be to artificially limit its potential. Some examples of play with food are listed in Table 3 (on pages 41-44), but often natural resources offer the most exciting and engaging resources and also avoid the issue of waste. With a whetted appetite, the purpose of this list is to inspire more fun-filled play and learning. So get playing and give your senses a work out!

Practical tips for minimising problems

Mess

Not all sensory-rich play is messy but for most practitioners and parents, this is what sticks in their mind. Many adults struggle with the mess associated with play and therefore may unwittingly limit how often it is available or the environment in which it is offered to children. Clearly both common sense and safety need to prevail but children's creativity and natural desire to explore and create are likely to be artificially constrained if they are concerned about the need to avoid mess. A balance is needed and hopefully the following simple ideas provide some practical approaches for achieving this.

Achieving a balance with messy play

- Preparation to minimise or manage mess, e.g.
  - Appropriate flooring and covers for tables
  - Old clothes or protective clothing
  - Playing outdoors instead of inside to minimise the impact of mess
  - Providing child-sized brooms, dust pans and brushes for children to take responsibility themselves (and support to help them in doing so)
  - Labelling storage containers and ensuring these are accessible so that children can tidy up after play
  - Agreeing together rules (if needed) on playing (especially using a hosepipe!) and tidying up
  - Appropriate storage to minimise damage and pollution, etc.

Table 3: Other sensory play resources

Product	Activities and sensory focus
Apple sauce	• Dollop onto a flat surface for mark making. • Use for a 'Guess the Taste' game. (Introduce other sauces such as honey or mint sauce). • Play a 'Guess the Smell' game. • Make pictures with fingers and other objects to 'draw' through the sauce.
Biodegradable packing 'peanuts'	• Squeeze these in your hands, feeling them change shape. • Experiment with pressing them with heavy objects. • Add to water and watch them dissolve. • Mould into a sculpture.
Bread	• Knead and make bread, giving time to enjoy the smell of yeast, the feel as they knead and watch it rise. • Form into different shaped rolls. If appropriate let the children watch as the bread rises whilst cooking.
Bubble wrap	• Hide 'toys' such as bricks or musical instruments among the bubble wrap for a feely game. • Feel toys through the bubble wrap. How does it distort them? Can they guess what they are? • Lay bubble wrap out for children to stamp, roll and crawl over.
Cardboard box	• Provide a range of different sized boxes for all manner of play. • Use for storytelling. • Make houses, towers, cars etc. • Use for den making.
Cereal (ready brek/porridge/wheat biscuits)	• Create a gooey paste for painting or mark-making. • Create 'cement' for sculptures and building with, e.g. using wheat biscuits for bricks.
Compost	• Feel the crumbly texture. • Hide treasure and small-world characters in it for children to discover. • Dig and plant in a bag of compost. • Add water and mix to create concoctions or use for painting.
Couscous (dried)	• Offer with funnels, containers etc. for pouring and filling. • Put in plastic bottles to create musical shakers. Add glitter and sequins too. • Put couscous in a bowl with boiling water and fresh mint leaves (adult only) then cover with film or foil and watch the water disappear. Carefully remove the cover before offering for the children to make into couscous balls to eat. • Mix dry couscous into paint to add extra texture.
Clay	• Make imprints from natural objects like twigs, seedpods and leaves or toy car wheel tracks. • Mould to make sculptures or spiral pots. Add glitter etc.
Fruit tea leaves	• Write or draw pictures with fruit tea leaves by sprinkling over a glue outline on paper. Use coffee grounds instead. • Hide objects in loose tea leaves or add some to organza bags to create smelly bags. • Provide containers for pouring and filling. • Add water to see what happens.
Gloop made from corn flour	• Scoop some corn flour into a bowl for children to explore dry. • Encourage them to listen to it squeak as they squeeze it between their fingers. • Rub hands together to create a myriad of white lines and chalky prints from their hands.

Table 3: Other sensory play resources

Product	Activities and sensory focus
Gloop made from corn flour continued	• Gradually add some water for the children to explore how the consistency changes.
	• Add more and more water until very watery and then experiment with adding more corn flour to change the texture.
	• Drip the corn flour onto baking paper or tin foil to create pictures, lines and Jackson Pollock inspired prints.
	• Let children play with the corn flour over several hours and days to see how its consistency changes and to develop their ideas.
	• Add food colouring, glitter, sequins or natural essence such as fresh herbs or essential oils to increase interest.
	• Vary the quantities of corn flour and water to explore different consistencies and properties.
Ice and snow	• Make ice, play with it and taste! Children should use gloves if handling large pieces of ice.
	• Children can explore the ice with magnifying glasses and experiment with sprinkling salt on it to see what happens.
	• Make ice sculptures or amazing ice bowls by pressing edible flowers and leaves in water between two bowls before freezing.
	• Add food colouring to a block of ice and wait to see what happens.
	• Spot and collect icicles for measuring, drawing with or simply exploring.
	• Listen to the sound of dripping icicles.
	• Catch snowflakes on your tongue, taste them and feel them melt.
	• Looking at gorgeous snowflake shapes on a window pane.
	• Spot frost on blades of grass or spiders webs.
	• Use a range of moulds such as latex gloves, balloons, ice cube trays, chocolate box trays for making ice shapes.
	• Experiment with adding food colouring before freezing the ice and layering up in different colours as it freezes.
	• Tantalise taste buds by making edible ice cubes or ice lollies with juice or squash or make your own ice cream in a bag. (Follow the recipe in Nursery World Magazine, Out of School, October 2003.)
	• Explore snow outside and make snow angels.
	• Listen to the muffling effect of snow and how it changes sound.
	• Listen to the squeak of footprints on snow.
	• Add food colouring to snow and watch what happens.
Icing (ready/homemade)	• Roll into 'sausage' shapes and letters, print patterns on and use with cutters etc.
	• Add food colouring and vanilla or peppermint essence to change the smell and appearance.
	• Add fresh herb leaves like mint to create different effects when rolled.
	• Make pots from rolled 'sausages' of icing.
Jelly	• Add fruit, edible flowers and herb leaves to create a work of art.
	• Use sieves to experiment with pushing the jelly through.
	• Make different shapes using moulds, chocolate box trays and metal, wooden and plastic spoons.
	• Add aquatic animals to blue jelly to play with.
Material scraps (of different textures)	• Use pieces of fabric and fabric remnants (old sheets, carpet, silk, velvet, hessian).
	• Cut them into strips or small squares and put in bags or a treasure chest for children to discover or feel with their eyes closed.
	• Cut an assortment of different textured fabric into strips for threading and weaving with.

Table 3: Other sensory play resources

Product	Activities and sensory focus
Paint	• Paint on a large scale with hands, feet, rolls of wallpaper or large sheets of paper. • Dollop paint onto a large sheet of paper outside and ride vehicles, (toy and real), through the paint to create tyre tracks. • Pour thick paint into two shallow containers then invite the children to walk, run, skip and jump in their wellingtons through the paint, leaving patterns across the paper. • Offer a variety of different painting mediums, e.g. old roll-on deodorants (washed and filled with paint), plant mister sprays, rollers, toothbrushes, a range of brushes, vegetables and fruit cut in half to make prints with. • Add sand, dried couscous etc. to paint to give it texture. • Explore pattern making with your finger, dripping and splashing. • Line the base of a shallow tray with a safety mirror to see reflections when playing with paint. Add sequins or objects to the paint. • Use feet instead of hands or slightly warm the paint in the microwave prior to use. (Check temperature before use). • Pour paint from a watering can, jug, or bottle from high up onto large sheets of paper and experiment with mark-making. • Add washing-up liquid to paint to give it a glossy look.
'Paper' mud	• Layer a fresh roll of toilet paper in a large bowl, sprinkle grated soap over this and add warm water. Leave over night to form modelling dough. • Use to make sculptures and models.
Pasta (dried)	• Provide shallow or deep containers for play with dried pasta. • Offer string for threading. • Provide different coloured paint for painting penne or tube pasta and use for pattern making, sequencing, sorting or creating necklaces. • Mix with dried rice or sand for extra interest. • Stick to card or paper with glue to create pictures. • Put three different types of pasta in different containers, e.g. spaghetti, tubes and shells, for the children to sort, play with, pour and fill containers and compare sounds. • Experiment with sounds by making mini-instruments. Make shakers from washed empty yoghurt pots. • Add water to increase play potential or change the consistency.
Pastry dough	• Add fresh herbs such as basil, cheese or marmite to pastry to add flavour. • Add sesame seeds, etc to add texture and taste. • Texture could also be added in the form of oats, sawdust etc. • Roll into shapes or alphabet 'sausages'. • Use with cutters or experiment with different prints.
Plasticine	• Offer all one colour and then a mix of colours to see the effect upon play.
Plaster (flour and water)	• Mix some plaster in a washing up bowl or use plaster and gradually add water – remembering not to play for too long or the mixture will set. Wash hands well with soap and water after!
Playdough	• Provide some food colouring and water to see what happens when kneaded with the dough. • Form 'sausage letters' or shapes with rolled dough. • Use as pretend food or to create sculptures. • Add scent to the mixture, e.g. vanilla essence to provide interest. • Chop up basil, coriander or mint leaves and add to the mixture. This will add colour, smell and interest but will need to be kept in the fridge.

Table 3: Other sensory play resources

Product	Activities and sensory focus
Playdough continued	• Use natural seedpods and leaves to make imprints with. • Add sequins, glitter or tiny shells to the dough while moulding. • Change the colour or smell to enhance a current topic or activity. • Offer the dough in lots of different colours to encourage colour mixing and to see if this inspires a different type of play.
Rice (dried)	• Provide a range of spoons, containers and funnels for pouring, filling, transporting, etc. • Provide black card and glue for creating pictures with the rice. • Mix into paint to add texture for painting. • Put in plastic bottles to create musical shakers or cut two rectangles of card and stick three sides together before half filling with rice. Secure the final side and rock from side to side to create the sound of the sea.
Shaving foam	• Squirt onto a surface for mark-making with fingers or a selection of objects. • Add essential oils or food colouring. • Provide glitter, sequins and powder paint to add to squirted foam for mixing and pattern-making. • Add sand, pea shingle, dried rice or couscous for extra texture. • Play on a safety mirror to add to the sensory focus or surprise.
Shredded paper and packaging	• Offer foam, shredded paper, cardboard or other packaging materials for children to feel. • Hide objects in the packing material to create feely bags and boxes. • Fill a giant-sized box for children to crawl in and explore or find objects. • Add essential oils to the paper and allow them to diffuse. • Encourage children to guess the smells and help choose which oils to use and mix. • Add bubble wrap to increase noise potential and add further textures. • Experiment with biodegradable packing 'peanuts', pressing them between fingers, adding to water or rolling in sand.
Soapflakes	• Mix two cups of soapflakes with half a cup of hot water. Make together and talk about what the children think will happen. • Add paint powder if wished and talk about how children think it will change.
Wallpaper paste	• Make up the paste for exploring with hands, fingers or feet. Ensure that it is non-fungicidal. • Add shingle or glitter for textural/visual interest.
Washing up liquid and water	• Use for bubble making, hiding objects in, washing up or bathing baby dolls. Add straws for blowing. • Experiment with unusual bubble blowers such as funnels, tubing, racquets or plastic netting. • Add small-world creatures to extend play. • Add a tiny amount of food colouring or glitter to the bubbles.
Wood shavings	• Hide things for children to find in a container of wood shavings. (Check toxin free). • Smell and play with the curly cork screws of wood.

NB: Always check for possible allergies and supervise play.

a choking hazard; free from sharp edges; and are not falling apart or broken. Similarly select items for heuristic play and loose parts play having regard to safety issues. A common sense approach involves balancing the need to manage risk whilst still offering children challenging and stimulating environments. Most children will naturally undertake their own subconscious risk assessments. Conversely children who are bored and under-stimulated can subvert their environment to create the challenge and stimulation that they desire.

Inclusion

- When planning sensory-rich experiences for children think about all the senses, rather than just the visual and auditory sense that toys tend to appeal to. It is not necessary for each experience to appeal to as many of the senses as possible. In fact, as we will see in chapter four for some children this play with all the senses can be overwhelming. However, do be aware of which senses are being catered for so as not to miss some out.
- Be sensitive to the fact that some children (and adults) have a strong dislike of getting messy or touching certain materials. It is important to respect this and wherever possible plan for their inclusion, e.g. by using spoons or sticks to play with sand, etc.

Other issues

Offering foodstuffs to children for sensory play is a matter of personal view and something that divides opinion. The argument for including foodstuffs cites the extra sensory interest and easy access within the home. The argument against states that it encourages faddy eating and playing with food at meal times, which is distasteful when there are people starving in the world. A middle ground might be to offer uncooked food that is past its sell by date, such as rice, pasta or couscous. However, if you've never tried natural materials like seedpods, petals and twigs, give it a go as you may be surprised by their amazing play potential.

- Observing children's play to guide what resources you offer and where, e.g. if observations reveal that the reason for mess in the water tray is that children are trying to access water to play with the sand then take positive steps to proactively support this exploration. E.g. by moving the two resources nearer to each other; or if you want to retain them as two distinct mediums; offering two areas for sand, one with and one without water; or rotating offering water next to the sand so that children can get the opportunity to explore both mediums.
- Involving parents in messy play can help them understand its benefits and curriculum links and reinforce the need for children being dressed appropriately, i.e. not in their best clothes.
- Giving practitioners the chance to play and explore themselves can help them see these resources with child-like eyes.

Safety

- Children's safety is of paramount concern. Before offering sand, water, mud etc. to children to play with ensure that you have checked for potential pollutants. Better still offer sand or soil play in sealed covered containers, protected from animal interference. Regularly change the still water in water tables to avoid contamination. Carefully check the contents of treasure baskets to ensure they are: not small enough to cause

Sensory play and special educational needs

Since all learning in the brain ultimately stems from sensory stimulation, the importance of our senses and of providing ample and appropriate opportunities for stimulation are apparent. For some children with special educational needs (SEN), sensory stimulation can present itself in unusual ways, which in turn affects children's knowledge and interpretation of the world. A learning environment rich in sensory experiences can benefit all children, provided we have a good understanding of their particular sensory needs, including which stimuli to avoid. With no two children the same it is not possible to cover sensory stimulation and SEN in detail. However, this chapter seeks to flag up some challenges and their implications for children and in so doing, increase knowledge and understanding.

As we discovered in the introduction, the importance of sensory play traces back to our miraculous brain. Typically, when a child learns something the information from the environment, gained through their senses, travels through the central nervous system to the brain to be analysed. A message is sent to the appropriate part of the body and an action results, be it 'let go', if holding a hot pan, or 'continue licking' if enjoying a tasty ice cream. If operating efficiently, a cycle develops between the sensory stimulus, mind and body, with feedback from each stage forming a fundamental part of the learning process (Christine Macyntyre, 2010). For many children (and adults) with SEN, sensory stimulation gives rise to significant challenges as well as benefits:

Lack of feedback

Some children with SEN experience problems when a lack of feedback makes it difficult to learn from situations, so they repeat the same mistakes or need to re-learn every movement as though for the first time. Most of us take this for granted when learning complex actions like walking, riding a bike, swimming or writing. Once mastered, these action are consigned to our subconscious and we do not need to think about them.

 Activity

Imagine how difficult daily functions might be and how much time it would take if you had to re-learn everything. What effect might this have on your confidence, ability to do something quickly, or focus and concentrate?

Lack of integration

Another problem arises when the senses do not all act together as they should, known as sensory integration (A. Jean Ayres, 1972). Without ever being aware of it, our complex brains pull together sensory feedback from numerous sources to give a complete 'picture'. Sight and touch are the two most important senses in helping us interpret information about the world around us. Indeed a child's exploring fingers have been described as an extension to their eyes (John Brierley, 1994) and a 'reality' check to our understanding. In most children with autism and Down's syndrome the visual sense features more prominently, with research identifying more activity in these parts of the brain and less in the frontal cortex – responsible for problem solving and thinking. Many people with SEN may only be able to receive and process information from one source at a time, making it difficult to make sense of the world. This can also result in delays in processing information, with a knock-on effect on comprehension, and reinforces their need for time to focus.

Over and under stimulation

Children with SEN, and particularly autism, are often more sensitive to sensory stimulation, experiencing either over (hyper) sensitivity or under (hypo) sensitivity to stimuli. This can relate to any of the senses, with hyperstimulation expressed as constant interference, even leading to actual pain from noise, light, touch, taste etc. In some children, hypersensitivity can mean they are painfully sensitive

to touch, and need a lot of personal space. In others the trigger may be noise, smells or taste, or a combination of these as this condition is rarely as simplistic as being confined to a single sense. An example of this is some people's repulsion at the smell of being touched (see **Activity** below). Many children can experience hypersensitivity for one sense and hyposensitivity with another. For others the degree of sensitivity and indeed whether it is hyper or hypo can actually change, making it very difficult to plan for their needs.

 ## Activity

Imagine what it might be like to be so sensitive to the sense of smell that if your clothes are touched the revulsion of the smell is so great that you have to remove the clothes and not wear them again until washed. This is the experience of Vicky; a girl hypersensitive to sounds, smell and touch (Olga Bogdashina, 2003, p.61). For Vicky it is essential for carers to be aware of, understand the extent of her repulsion and respect her coping mechanisms. Now try to imagine equivalent responses for the other senses.

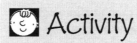 ## Activity

Think about how we can adapt children's play and learning environments to better meet the needs of all children. For example, provide private spaces and dens to offer quiet, calm and refuge for some; restructure the day to give children adequate time; offer play opportunities outdoors.

For children in the same environment there is great scope for conflict given that some children need (or are typically used to) loud noise, whilst others are fearful of this for the pain that it causes. Many potential sources of pain, discomfort, fear and distraction may not be obvious to practitioners, as they do not affect them. For example, problems caused by a profusion of colours, the otherwise imperceptible flicker of a fluorescent light; shrill sounds, or simply too many simultaneous sounds; the use of particular, pungent smelling, cleaning materials; or the fact that trying new textured foods, or mixing foods of different textures, may cause concern for a child hypersensitive to touch. Within an early years or primary school environment, this can disrupt children's involvement and learning 'by stealth' as we may be completely unaware of potential distractions.

Focus on detail

With their bodies constantly bombarded by sensory stimuli, some children with SEN, particularly those on the autistic spectrum, may tend to focus on particular details rather than 'seeing the bigger picture'. Some have described the characteristics of autism – problems with communication and language, social and emotional difficulties and imagination, as symptoms of over- or under- sensory stimulation, and coping mechanisms to deal with these sensory problems. For example, one autistic child likened daily life to an untuned radio (see activity overleaf). When tuned in he was able to engage in satisfying human interactions, but when fuzzy he would avoid such interactions (Olga Bogdashina, 2003).

Activity

Turn on the radio and adjust the frequency so that you hear lots of background noise, but not any particular station properly. Now imagine that you are sat in a room and you can hear a chair move or a rubber drop on the floor in another room. How easy would it be for you to concentrate on what somebody is saying to you? Now imagine that the radio station keeps tuning in and out of focus so that one minute it is crystal clear and the next blurry, how difficult would it be to understand all the instructions for a task or the plot of a story? How can we support all children, but particularly those experiencing hyper- or hypo-sensitivity, to be more included?

Donna Williams, an acclaimed autistic author describes how "*her problem in infancy was not so much that she did not understand the world, but that she could not stand it, because she was so often bombarded with an overload of sensory information*"(Theo Peters in: Olga Bogdashina, 2003, p.14). For those of us lucky enough to experience sensory stimulation typically, it is difficult to understand the significance of what might appear very trivial actions. Take a pencil precariously balanced on the edge of a table and a child with hyper-hearing focused intently on the pencil, unable to concentrate on anything else for fear of the painful noise that it will make if allowed to drop to the floor (Marc Fleisher, 2001). Or imagine having hearing which is like a microphone, picking up every scrap of noise, and having the choice of being overwhelmed or turning it off (Temple Grandin in: Olga Bogashina, 2003, p.13). With these examples in mind, it is easy to understand just how challenging a typical early years setting or primary school might be. With lots of noise, visual stimuli and bustling activities, for some children quiet space and time spent can represent a welcome respite.

Positive action

Regardless of SEN, many children find paying attention a key challenge. A number of proactive strategies can help, such as allowing the use of sensory-rich resources to provide feedback; providing quiet spaces to sit in calmly and take time out; minimising other distractions; and using attractive resources to encourage less-preferred activities (Christine Mcintyre, 2005). As with all children, it is a case of understanding each individual to discover the types of resources or activities that will best captivate them. Appropriate sensory stimulation increases children's concentration and focus, helping them to self-occupy. It can also develop muscle tone and is inclusive because there are no right or wrong ways of playing, appealing to children with different learning styles and abilities. For a child who needs proprioceptive feedback – from touching ribbons or other tactile resources – in order to sit still, this needs to be understood in the same way that a pair of spectacles or a wheelchair would be. Many children develop stims (self-stimulations) like flapping their arms or rocking. These individual coping mechanisms help them deal with the problem, giving respite from a world of bombardment. If inappropriate, children can be helped to develop more socially acceptable coping mechanisms with professional support, and should not be denied this opportunity for self-expression.

Many children with autism benefit from being in a 'just right' state, where they are neither over-nor under-stimulated. Accessing a 'diet' of appropriate sensory-rich play and learning opportunities throughout the day can help children achieve this (Patricia Wilbarger and Julia Wilbarger, 1991). A sensory room, low-cost 'sensory den', ball pool, gym or aqua pool are great for providing a real sensory workout or 'main meal'. But sensory stimulation also needs to take place in between these times, in non-specialised environments, involving little or no specialist planning or provision. 'Sensory snacks' are opportunities for children to play with sensory–rich resources *in situ*, making them perfect for use in early years settings, mainstream schools and in the home. So what might a sensory-rich learning environment look like in practice?

The sensory room – a sensory 'main meal'

The sensory room (or a lower-cost smaller/portable version) is an all-singing, all-dancing sensory environment with much to offer children with SEN. The coloured lights, dark and calm environment, sounds and sights of bubbles and water all have a key role to play and can be controlled to make a real difference to children's lives, providing a respite from constant sensory overload. Like aqua pools and gyms, this all-encompassing provision can offer large-scale sensory experiences, albeit at a price and on a scale that may limit provision to specialist schools.

Although multi-sensory by name, the resources in a typical sensory room can be predominantly plastic or fabric, offering little in the way of sensory stimulation to the tactile sense, so this may be something to consider if the children who will be accessing the room benefit from tactile stimulation.

Treasure baskets – a 'sensory snack'

A treasure basket is an example of a sensory-rich and highly portable resource, making it a perfect 'sensory snack'. Within an enabling environment children can investigate objects, experiment, or be guided with activities. The sensory stimulation and hands-on approach is great for brain and memory development, gross and fine motor skills and strength. With no right or wrong ways of playing, they can appeal to children with different learning styles and abilities.

To avoid sensory overload some children may need to be offered the 'treasures' individually or just a few at a time. Other children may need heavy items to be removed (to avoid potential danger from throwing) or more robust alternatives to be provided instead. Still others may need to be supported in moving play on to avoid overly repetitive play.

The outdoor environment – a 'main meal' or 'sensory snack'

With an emphasis upon access to play opportunities outdoors, making a distinction between formal learning indoors and 'running around' outdoors would be to seriously limit the real play and learning potential of the outdoor environment, marginalising it as simply a place to 'let off steam'. With flexibility, the outdoor environment can come to offer both a 'sensory snack' and 'main meal', avoiding much of the sensory overload likely to be so difficult for children with sensory processing problems.

A study of the effects of green space upon mood and self esteem revealed that even five minutes exposure generated positive effects, with the presence of water increasing this still further. Research also suggests that 'exposure to greenery' benefits children's ability to pay attention, with children with ADHD (Attention Deficit Hyperactivity Disorder) significantly reducing their symptoms. Interestingly, the greener the environment, the greater the change was evident (*American Journal of Public Health*, September 2004; Barton, J & Pretty, J. 2010). Follow-up studies of children with ADHD taken on a 20-minute walk in the park revealed similar elevated attention levels to a dose of Ritalin. Furthermore, simply providing views of green areas increased attention and reduced impulsiveness among those without ADHD, particularly girls – proof of the positive benefits of access to a sensory-rich environment (*Montessori International*, April-June 2011).

In a research project carried out by Redcliffe Children's Centre in Bristol six children aged three to four years with wide ranging additional needs were taken on weekly visits to a wild space in a local wood. Over a period of nine months the challenge, calm, space, freedom from loud noises and other sensory irritants, as well as the changing environment increased children's confidence, communication, cognitive development and attitude to risk. "*The forest environment seemed a wonderful place to stimulate all of the senses in a natural and balanced way. Sensory integration appeared to work very effectively and all children showed that they were able to process whether a sensation was from their own body or from the environment*" (Jeanette Hill, EECERA, 2010).

Implications for adults

Staff too, at Redcliffe experienced a learning journey, gaining a better understanding of children's capabilities and pushing the boundaries of what they felt was acceptable in terms of risk and challenge. While watching a child struggle to scale a hill, practitioners questioned the process, but once achieved, the pride, satisfaction and pure joy of the child convinced them of the value of children experiencing challenge and risk. An observation of teenagers playing with a treasure basket in a special school revealed similarly surprising results. The children freely engaged with the objects and to the surprise of practitioners, examples of sensory regulation (using objects to achieve a 'just right' state) and imaginative play emerged. One boy discovered a tin designed to look like a mini-postbox and proceeded to put objects in it saying he was posting them. He then got into the role of a postman, making deliveries to people around the room. Imaginary play and using an object to represent something else are not typically associated with children on the autistic spectrum and so was particularly noteworthy for the practitioners observing this session.

Examples like these emphasise the importance of the senses and the fact that some children's responses to sensory stimulation can impact upon their ability to participate in play and learning. Equipped with this knowledge we can better understand and effectively plan for children's needs, raising our expectations of what children with SEN can achieve within an enabling environment. Sensory resources like a treasure basket can also be a valuable aid in identifying potential problems.

Practical tips

- Give clear and simple instructions.
- Break down activities into very simple stages, e.g. with a treasure basket initially offer just a couple of items. Base your selection upon your knowledge of their likes and dislikes. Alternatively, offer first as part of a structured activity for children to potentially access later for free play.
- Increase the complexity of actions/activities in minute stages and only if and when appropriate to do so.
- Don't assume that you can build upon previous play and learning. This may never be possible and could be frustrating or lower self-esteem.
- Be open-minded about your expectations, to avoid these limiting outcomes.
- Give adequate time for children to think, explore and become accustomed.
- Provide appropriate visual or auditory cues, e.g. traffic lights or an egg timer, to prepare children for what is expected, what will happen, when it will happen and when it will stop.
- Observe children to understand what sort of sensory stimulations they enjoy and those they find difficult. Base activities on your knowledge, for example visual activities for those who enjoy and benefit from a visual focus.
- Provide spaces and opportunities for meeting children's different needs, be it through stimulation or quiet and calm.
- Respect children's needs and responses and find out more to try to understand what they might be experiencing, rather than judging from our very different perspective.
- Be aware of typical developmental milestones that may help flag up potential problems to raise with healthcare professionals.
- Provide individual 'work stations' for children to play and explore in, e.g. using separate trays, bowls or even an area delineated by a cloth on the floor. This can avoid potential conflicts and give children adequate space.
- Try offering a favourite toy next to another less popular resource like sand, to encourage the child to experiment.
- If appropriate, only offer a favourite toy or experience after the child has tried out an activity.

Take this example of four babies under eight months sat around a treasure basket. Three of the four were eager, excited and exploring the objects, while the fourth, a very passive baby, did not take part. She was later diagnosed with severe developmental delay (Katrin Stroh et al., 2008).

Since all learning starts with our senses, sensory-rich play opportunities should be a natural ingredient in any enabling environment. As we discovered in chapter three, for typically developed children, multi-sensory play is great. However, for children with SEN we need to be aware of the very different impacts of sensory stimulation to ensure that with careful support we can help give children 'the best start in life' as well as lots of fun!

Curriculum links

In 2012 the Statutory Framework for the EYFS was published and the areas of learning for the early years sector, and ultimately children, became clearer. Although the word 'play' itself does not feature prominently, and the emphasis upon Mathematics, teaching and school readiness signal a closer alignment with Key Stage 1, for the youngest children much of the play-based ethos remains intact. A reduction in early learning goals from 69 to 17 eases the burden of paperwork and the importance of the partnership between practitioners and parents has been reinvigorated. The six areas of learning and development have been replaced with three **prime** areas of Personal, Social and Emotional Development, Communication and Language and Physical Development. Literacy, Mathematics, Understanding the World and Expressive Arts and Design now form four **specific** areas of learning and development. "*Practitioners working with the youngest children are expected to focus strongly on the three prime areas.* " (Department for Education, July 2011). For older children the balance shifts towards 'a more equal focus on all seven areas of learning'. This recognises the crucial role played by these lynchpins in the development of 'well rounded' children and ultimately accessing life's opportunities.

For many practitioners the downplaying and separation of literacy from communication and language is particularly welcome, as is recognition of the importance of physical development for developing tool use and pencil control. Conversely the replacement of problem solving, reasoning and numeracy (so abundant in children's every day explorations and play) with the much more narrowly focussed, and potentially less exciting Mathematics is (personally speaking) a retrograde step. That said, underlying the new EYFS is recognition of the different ways that children learn and the importance of the following three characteristics of effective learning:

- Playing and exploring
- Active learning
- Creating and thinking critically.

All three of these characteristics have a strong synergy with sensory play and represent key strengths in offsetting not just the greater emphasis upon school readiness but also the current debate about increasing practitioner/child ratios.

A key challenge can be justifying to parents the value of children's play, especially messy play. The Statutory EYFS (Department for Education, 2012) attaches great importance to the effective and meaningful engagement of parents recognising that this is critical to the life opportunities of future generations. As the following snapshots reveal, although not curriculum-led, deeply absorbing play provides real curricular outputs without the need for expensive or specialist equipment that might alienate some. As such, sensory-rich play is a perfect vehicle for engaging parents in quality play and interactions with their children and fostering an understanding of the benefits of play. The best learning is relevant, real and rooted in children's interests and existing knowledge. This definitely doesn't involve treating different aspects of the curriculum in isolation, but it is helpful to consider how sensory play can contribute to each of the prime areas, specific areas of learning and development and Early Learning Goals (identified in bold).

Prime areas

Personal, social and emotional development (PSED)

Sand, mud, water, natural resources and a whole raft of other objects typically found in a treasure basket or 'loose parts' play are perfect for fostering **self-confidence and self-awareness; managing feelings and behaviour; and making relationships**. This is true for children across the ages as the resources are all open-ended and there are no right or wrong ways of playing with them, making them very inclusive and empowering. Watch a child deeply engrossed in play and we gain an insight into their personality, interest and schemas (repeated patterns of behaviour). Sustained focus can be indicative of children's contented exploration, problem solving and testing of ideas and theories, common occurrences in sensory play. It can contribute to their emotional wellbeing and

give meaning to a whole host of words like: soft and hard, hot and cold, heavy and light, rough and smooth, big and small. Without actually experiencing these concepts a child cannot meaningfully put a name to them. Some children respond to these resources in very different ways, for example babies and young children may babble as they play and explore, appearing to commentate on their play. Others play in silence, possibly because they are focussing so intently on their play. The unusualness of the resources and element of surprise about what they will do can inspire language and critical thinking. It can also produce spontaneous and meaningful writing or mark-making, like the children who developed perfume and wine labels for their bottled concoctions.

 Activity

Pretend that you are talking to someone from a tropical country who has never left their climate. Try to describe different types of weather to them. Reflect upon how hard this is to do; how well they could ever grasp something like snow without actually experiencing it; and how much time and words experiences replace?

understanding of themselves and what they can do. If used appropriately this is especially relevant for children with sensory perception difficulties.

Without branding to artificially restrict play, children of markedly different ages (or developmental levels) can happily play side by side, each playing and exploring in a different, yet age-appropriate way. This can also give rise to wonderful moments of peer mentoring, where a peer helps extend another child's learning, as the four year old did when they suggested adding water to the sand in the wire eggcup in chapter three. These open-ended resources as well as other children at play, appear to help take children to the zone of proximal development.

Communication and language (CL)

The open-ended nature of most sensory play is great for promoting **listening and attention**; enhancing **understanding** and **encouraging speaking**. With adults sometimes rushing for children to meet literacy milestones, it's worth noting that sensory-rich experiences like these are a necessary pre-cursor to reading and writing. They

Physical development (PD)

Play with highly malleable, open-ended resources is great for developing fine and gross motor skills as well as strength, key aspects of **moving and handling** and **self-care**. As even very young babies sit absorbed in play with a treasure basket they are developing their back, shoulder and arm muscles, building strength and coordination and hardwiring their brains for learning. Unlike adults, children's play is often full-bodied and therefore their learning is too. Consider the challenge of mark-making in dry or wet sand, gloop or mud. Splashing in muddy puddles or stretching to climb a tree. Squeezing sand or mud between fingers or painting with a fat brush. Collecting minibeasts or kneading pastry or dough. All these actions

The importance of exploration is still recognised by its inclusion as a characteristic of effective teaching. Problem solving lies at the heart of countless sensory-rich play experiences. It helps give meaning to mathematics and science as well as providing rich fodder for language and communication. Due in large part to the open-endedness of sensory play materials, the behaviour and properties of resources throws up numerous opportunities for disequilibrium, surprise, and the investigation of cause and effect, trial and error, pattern, volume and so much more. Water or sand play can help bring numeracy to life with hands on challenges like "How many small pots of water are needed to fill a large pot?" Or "How many pots of water do you need to sink the paper boat?" This practical, hands-on approach is essential and provides for deeply satisfying experiences. With most of this play being child-initiated, children show amazing concentration as they focus on the challenge they have presumably set themself: be it how to create a car from 'loose parts'; how to get a long heavy dog chain into a small pot; or how to fit packing 'peanuts' into a tin.

require wide-ranging physical skill and mastery, but above all are enriching and fun. On a practical note, the messy or natural dimension of sensory play also helps promote positive self-care, such as the washing of hands!

Specific areas

Literacy (L)

This new area of learning and development focuses on **reading** and **writing**. As several of the play scenarios will show, sensory-rich play and resources have a great role to play in making mark-making meaningful and fun. The provision of stimulating reading resources – both fact and fiction – as well as cosy, secret places to enjoy these in, will also support reading.

Mathematics (M)

The focus on Mathematics marks a move away from problem solving and reasoning to a closer alignment with Key Stage 1.

Understanding the world (UW)

Sand, mud, water, natural resources and the outdoor environment are great for introducing the characteristics of materials, promoting questions like: "What things are?", "What they're made of?", "Where do they come from?", "What are they used for?" and so on. Through play with a treasure basket children come to understand the properties of resources and how these change; master the use of tools; and enter a world of hands-on scientific discovery. Depending upon the objects they can also be used to introduce **people and communities** and **the world** in a hands-on inspirational way. **Technology** too can be seamlessly linked to sensory-rich play, with stimulating resources and space inspiring investigation and meaningful use.

Expressive arts and design (EAD)

Focusing on **exploring and using media and materials** and **being imaginative**, the lack of a right or wrong way of playing

Play snapshot

Eight-month-old baby, shallow sand tray and deeper tray on the floor, both filled with purple coloured sand.

Baby A started at the shallow tray and began spooning sand using the teaspoon, putting the handle end of the spoon in her mouth and then discovered that a tiny amount of the sand had stuck to the wet part of the spoon, so she continued spooning sand and putting the handle end in her mouth. She transferred from one tray to another whilst continuing using the teaspoon.

I added brushes, she looked at these, discarded them and continued using the teaspoon, holding the spoon end and spooning with the handle end. Baby A ignored other children crawling through the sand tray and continued spooning.

Reflection: Baby A is discovering about cause and effect, thermic properties (metal things warm up if held), and that sand sticks to wet things (UW & MD). She is developing hand-eye coordination, fine motor skills and amazing concentration and focus (PD & PSED). We can observe a potential preference for metal objects, and purposeful decision-making and use of tools (PSED & UW).

Play snapshot

Boy aged two years eight months, rarely plays with sand or vocalises during play.

Child B spent 10 minutes using a teaspoon to fill a small metal bowl and half a tea infuser with sand. After filling the bowl he smoothed the sand, patted it, and then used the brush to brush the sand. He did this very carefully with good fine motor control. His play then changed to pretend play and he started to comment on his own play. He filled the metal eggcup with sand saying "Wait a minute need egg". Then filling the pan with sand and saying "making tea now".

Child B brushed sand off the sides of the sand tray repeating "brush, brush, brush", then singing "brush, brush, brush it off, it clean now, it not got any sand on it anymore".

Child B started burying objects saying "where's it gone?" then finding it, saying "here it is".

Reflection: This child shows great manual dexterity and fine motor skills (CL, PD). His communication and language skills are evident. He is deeply focused for over an hour playing with a resource he never normally plays with (PSED). He uses the objects for domestic role-play and develops his own song and hiding game (EAD). He shows an understanding of cause and effect and good social skills (MD, UW & PSED).

with sensory-rich resources makes them great for encouraging creativity. In a world where so many toys have limited ways of being used, open-ended resources can inspire music making, art, games and role-play. But this is to underplay their creative potential. As White explains: "*materials that can be transformed by combining or mixing make for especially fascinating and productive play. When materials can be collected, handled, manipulated and moved around, their play value is further enhanced, allowing children to mould and create their play environment*" (Jan White, 2011 p.52).

Snapshots of play

Using sensory play as a tool it is possible to move beyond curriculum divisions and provide times:

- For quiet reflection, achievement and focus

- To nurture communication and mark-making
- To spark problem solving and mathematical investigation
- To discover about the world, as well as the properties and wonders of science
- To use their bodies with purpose
- To inspire creativity and role play.

As areas of learning do not take place in silos, but rather in a seamless and interlinked way the above snapshots of play provide some examples of this in action.

Sessions like these emphasise the importance of giving children time and space to solve their own challenges through trial and error. It also highlights the potential play value of mess!

Play snapshot

Boy aged three years playing on a busy exhibition stand.

Child F played happily with a treasure basket for 30 minutes or more before spying a drawer containing dried rice. He rummaged through the basket and proceeded to use a large metal spoon to fill a mini-flower pot with dried rice. After refilling the pot numerous times he noticed the red carpet covered with white rice and the hole in the bottom of the pot. Unprompted, he started rummaging through the basket and after much trial and error he discovered that the nail brush was perfect for moving the rice. His clearing up was momentarily put on hold when he noticed the patterns he was creating with the brush and explored this further. He then continued tidying the rice away using the treasure basket objects.

Refection: In this child-led session the child explored problem solving, and trial and error. He appeared to pursue his own goals – of getting the rice out of the drawer, filling the pot, making patterns and clearing up the rice (PSED, PD, MD). He demonstrated great focus and concentration and did not appear to be phased by the 'messy problem' that he'd created (PSED). He showed great creativity through the approach he applied to 'the challenge' and in the patterns that he created (EAD). He showed a good understanding and use of tools and great fine and gross motor skills, hand eye coordination and manipulation (UW & PD). No verbal communication was used, but his body language appeared to convey to both adults present that he was happy and 'in control' (PSED & CL).

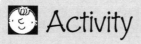 Activity

Observe one or more children playing with open-ended resources like those listed in chapter three. Simply watch what they do, how they play, what objects they use, and any language used? Record any areas that you feel you could support the child in extending their learning (on another occasion). List any surprises or learning points. How will this affect what you do or offer in the future?

The Tickell Review recognised that *"not enough credibility is given to how important it is for children to play and explore in order for them to develop communication, speaking and listening and social and emotional skills"* (Clare Tickell, March 2011). Sensory play provides an important mechanism for redressing this balance.

Observation and assessment

The new EYFS continues to recognise the importance of 'practitioners observing children on an ongoing basis, understanding their level of achievement, interests and learning styles, and shaping learning experiences for each child reflecting their observations'. This assessment should take place as part of ongoing interaction with children and be informed by feedback from parents and other adults who interact with the child. It is proposed that between the age of 24 and 36 months, children's progress in relation to the three prime areas should be reviewed and where progress is less than anticipated, a targeted plan be developed. This marks a key development in the relationship between practitioners and parents as a summary of this process is to be shared with parents. In the final term in which a child reaches age five, a second assessment process, the EYFS Profile is scheduled to take place. Children's development will be assessed in relation to the 17 early learning goals and three key characteristics of effective learning (see page 52).

Observations and sensory play

Like many other examples of quality play, sensory play is a great platform for carrying out ongoing observations. As the play snapshots illustrate, open-ended, sensory-rich resources provide ample scope for children to shape their own play and in doing so provide wonderful insights into different children's developmental levels, interests, schemas and thinking.

The same medium, whether it be a muddy puddle or pile of 'loose parts' objects, can evoke countless responses in different children and at different times. So the muddy puddle can help develop children's **focus and confidence** (Dare I step into a puddle when I can't see how deep it is?); **language and meaning** (as cold, seeping water and soggy wellies give real meaning to these words as well as forging longterm memories); **problem solving** (How deep is the puddle?/How can I find out if my wellies are high enough?); **understanding the world** (What will happen if I stir up the mud at the bottom?/Why is the bottom of a puddle different to the top?); **understanding my body and cause and effect** (How can I make the biggest splash?/How can I use the toe of my boot or a finger to make patterns in the mud?); and **creativity** (What jumping games can we create?/What's the imaginary story behind the puddle?).

Although none of these experiences are actually curriculum-led they can potentially deliver curriculum outputs. As Sylvia Dodds observes 'with skilled scaffolding by and shared thinking with an adult, whatever the focus of play for any age of child, there is potential for powerful learning' (Sylvia Dodds et al, 2009, p.154).

Play snapshot

Three children aged four years six months to four years nine months playing in the garden with a treasure basket. Only Child E (aged four years nine months) has played with this treasure basket before.

Child C fills up a pot using the large metal spoon. He turns it over and states "Look I made a sandcastle", banging the bottom to ensure it comes out. "Ta-da" he announces proudly.

Children D and E find the miniature terracotta pot in the purse. "Look ah it's a baby flower pot" says Child E. "It's small, look these ones are bigger" says D, comparing it to the flower pots in the garden. D fills up the terracotta pot and runs off around the grass area, she runs back to the sand pit and finds the sand has disappeared from the pot. "Hey. How that happen?" says D. "My sand all gone!", "It's got a hole in it D, that's why" says E. (Each of the children fill up the pot and run around the garden. When they get back to the sandpit they look to see who has the most sand left).

C picks up the metal eggcup and fills it up with sand. He lifts it up and the sand falls out. "Oh man, it's coming out!" so D says "You need some water." C gets some water and mixes it into the sand, and then puts the sand into the egg cup and says "It's staying there".

Reflection: This trio of children display excellent language for communication and thinking skills (CL). They make the links between big and little and are easily able to convey their ideas (MD & CL). They develop a game combining creativity with physical development (PD & EAD). They explore the properties of materials and science of cause, effect and change (UW & MD). They play with focus, appear confident in their own abilities and understanding and are adept at peer mentoring (PSED). This session captures children's amazing potential for problem solving (MD). An adult could so easily have stepped in and solved the issue of the hole, but given the space, time and opportunity to freely explore issues like these, children can discover the answers and adults learn just how much children understand about our complex world. First-hand experiences like these provide rich fodder for embedding learning as they are relevant, real and child-led.

The adult's role

Adults have a key role to play in providing children with safe yet stimulating resources and the space and time to fully and freely explore these. This is particularly true of sensory play given its association with messy play. Knowing when and when not to intervene in children's play, is a difficult decision that even the most experienced practitioners don't always get right.

If we take the time to observe children's play we gain a better understanding of their interests, developmental milestones and existing knowledge, and can better plan for their needs. This can also help us see the simplest of resources with fresh eyes. Watching an eight-month-old baby deeply engaged in exploring a natural coaster for an hour, or a three-year-old exploring sand with treasure basket objects for three hours, pinpoints something wonderful in action. The 2012 EYFS rightly places an emphasis upon children accessing a balance between adult- and child-led learning. But encouraging children to learn through self-discovery does not mean little or no adult input. The adult continues to play a vital, but not dominant role, in supporting children's learning in the following ways.

Safety

Listed first, not because it is adults' most important role, but so that we can move onto the more exciting aspects of play, safety is of course essential, but does not necessarily foster enriching play! Adults can provide the safest possible play environment and if it is bland, unchallenging, with limited play appeal children will naturally look at ways of altering it to make it more exciting. If you've ever seen children quickly tire of sliding down a slide in favour of attaching a rope to the top to climb up; climbing on top of the safety bars at a play area; or insisting on walking, running and jumping from a roadside wall, you will have seen this for yourself. For adults too this rings true with many childhood memories relaying exciting play experiences filled with challenge and potential risk, like wading in deep mud, building fires and climbing trees.

Many safety measures are common sense. When selecting objects for children's play, first check for sharp edges and loose parts, which could cause a potential choke hazard. Regularly check the condition of play materials replacing any that have become damaged. Wash or clean with soapy water, avoiding harsh chemicals that could in themselves present a health hazard. Consider how best to equip children with the necessary knowledge and skills to take responsibility themselves, like washing hands after play and before eating; clearing up spillages that may cause a slipping hazard; understanding what might happen if they take particular actions and how they can achieve the same thrill or effect in a safer way. Many children may subconsciously do this anyway, appraising play opportunities much like carrying out a risk assessment (Sue Palmer, 2010). In our risk adverse culture it is important to try to get the balance right rather than unwittingly removing all the fun, excitement and challenge of early learning in the name of safety.

Play snapshot

In a Forest School session, two girls spent time collecting short, sawn-off branches. They each found a tree stump to sit on and laid the lengths of wood on an upturned tree stump between them. With focus and energy they vigorously rolled the branches backwards and forwards, using a similar action to rolling pastry. I watched them deeply focused on the task in hand, waiting for a clearer insight into what they were doing. Their concentration was interrupted by a well-meaning practitioner asking "What are you doing girls?" They instantly stopped what they were doing and moved away from the logs, their play punctuated by the well-intended question. Having observed the play unfold I felt robbed, not knowing whether the children had been rolling pastry or something far removed. As for the children, one can only wonder what they felt and what might have been explored further.

Activity

Put your hand in a bag containing natural and household objects and feel them with your eyes closed. Write down any describing words that come to mind, like smooth, cold, hard etc. Chances are your list may include words like 'bristly', 'pointy', 'sharp', 'scary', not words generally associated with children's toys. It may also include words like 'exciting', 'wow' or as one practitioner in a training session described, a 'what can it be object?'. Repeat with a bag containing 'normal' toys. This time your list might include words like 'dull', 'safe' and 'boring'. These are just some of the words identified by practitioners on training courses, as they discover some of the magical awe, wonder and surprise of a treasure basket. It seems that the extra 'risk' of the unusual objects is rewarded by added excitement and surprise. It is a rare training session when someone does not peek at the treasure basket objects, unable to resist the urge to match what they are feeling to a word!

Reflection: Can you think of examples where children appear to have carried out their own 'assessment of risk' and changed action as a result? Next time you are faced with such a situation, (if safe to do so) take a moment to try to understand what the child is thinking before rushing in to take action.

Adult's vivid childhood play memories also provide a cautionary reminder of what children enjoy and ultimately remember. No adults recalled time spent playing on a play area with a guardian present. Instead, den making, playing in the woods, building fires, climbing trees and exploring free from adults were listed (Sue Gascoyne, January, 2010).

Activity

Try to think about a vivid play memory from your childhood. Was an adult present and if so what role did they play in shaping or supporting play? Were they just on the periphery or did they become actively engaged in play? Did they successfully join in or did it feel like they were trying to take over play? Consider whether this offers any insight into your role in children's play now.

Stimulating resources

When putting together collections of items for sensory-rich play it is important to pick these for their special interest and appeal to avoid creating a bland and sterile play environment. We discovered in chapter three that 'versatile, open-ended resources offer an enormous range of possibilities for play, can be used differently by every child and can be naturally transformed into anything the child wants them to be, developing symbolic thinking' (Jan White, 2011). As we saw with the four-year-old boy who chose only to engage in domestic role-play when offered open-ended resources, 'if the physical environment is over-defined and organised [like the play food perhaps] it limits the very play it is trying to encourage' (Jan White, 2011). The snapshot of an eight-month-old's play, in chapter five illustrates perfectly the role of the adult in providing stimulating resources. The sand was provided in both a shallow and deep tray and purple-coloured to provide extra interest and scope. During play the practitioner sensitively laid out more resources, in case these were of interest, but after a quick glance these were ignored by the child, without interrupting or changing the focus of play.

Space

Whilst much sensory-rich play involves exploration with the hands, meaningful interactions are also needed on a larger scale to provide full-bodied play and learning. The offer of sand, water and cornflour 'gloop' in small trays indoors is a valuable part of provision, but no substitute for children experiencing it in context in a meaningful and holistic way. Like the muddy puddle that magically appears after a downpour, or the dry patch of earth beneath the tree in an otherwise sodden garden, these natural scenarios are ripe for exploration and play. To maximise relevance and appeal plan the indoor and outdoor spaces with this in mind as well as planning trips to nearby environments. A quiet area of the garden (possibly sensory) provides a perfect spot for listening to birdsong; watching mobiles catch the light as they hang from branches; exploring natural objects;

enjoying a story or simply talking. Wild spaces are great for exploration and fantasy play; trees can lift the spirits; a den provides a secret space for reflection and being; and a sofa a cosy area to sit and relax.

Time

When reflecting upon the importance of time, Chilvers introduces the idea of children needing to 'wallow' – a wonderful word which truly conveys the dreamy essence of being a child (White, 2011). With increasingly mapped out lives, after-school clubs and organised activities, even children can face the pressure of limited time. For some, sensory-rich play is about losing yourself in the moment, which can be at odds with the timetabling of the day. The importance of time is aptly demonstrated by the three children aged four introduced in chapter five (see page 57). Had the practitioner hurried their thinking just think how different the outcomes might have been?

The children would have been the poorer without this opportunity for sustained shared thinking; the learning less concrete without hands-on experimentation and peer mentoring; and the practitioner unaware of the depth of their understanding.

Support

This brings us to the final key role of the adult, that of supporting children's play and thinking through sensitive facilitation. The EPPE report (Iram Siraj Blatchford et al., 2004) highlighted the importance of providing a balance between adult and child-led play, as well as group work and individual activities. This is as relevant to sensory play as play generally. Best practice was linked to ample opportunities for sustained interactions, providing challenge, and progressing children's thinking skills. Given appropriate spaces to foster such interactions, the time to fully explore new ideas, a supportive environment and sensitive adult, children's thinking was found to blossom and grow. The EPPE report identified several factors for encouraging deeply satisfying, memory-making play:

- enabling differentiation and challenge
- scaffolding of learning to 'build bridges' between a child's knowledge and what they are 'capable of knowing' (Iram Siraj Blatchford et al., 2004)
- the use of open-ended questions to stimulate and support rather than probe and test
- encouragement of new experiences
- adult's watching and listening before 'making their own mark.'

Sensory play has much to offer by way of learning and support, including its open-ended qualities that naturally differentiate and provide challenge; its ability to scaffold learning and provoke questions; the fact that it has no right or wrong ways of being played with; and the limitless opportunities for new experiences. Returning to those four-year-olds (page 57) who discovered first-hand about the properties of materials, cause and effect, gravity, language for communication and thinking and the satisfaction of solving problems, in case you're thinking an opportunity was missed for extending and scaffolding learning, fear not. The practitioner built on the learning observed by incorporating into her planning lots more opportunities for exploring different properties in a subsequent session.

If you have a particular interest, be it football, horses or 'Eastenders', you'll know that it is much easier sharing this interest with others who have the same passion. You don't need to explain the basics, as they understand these and the appeal. The same could be said of sensory play. We will be much more willing to see the sensory potential of simple things; create opportunities to provide sensory play; encourage others to try it; understand its benefits and what it could do for them, if we actually experience and enjoy sensory play ourselves.

For practitioners unsure of whether and when to intervene, the sensory play Continuum introduced in

'Sensory play in action' (see page 36), provides a useful framework for exploring adult's role in children's play.

In the first stage, when the child is freely playing with a treasure basket, the adult provides safe, yet stimulating resources; observes play when and if needed; provides support by intervening if a child is in difficulty or has had enough of play.

This child-led focus remains in stage two where the child chooses whether and what to combine, and the adult initially provides the selection of resources (based on interests) and observes play. It is in this most creative stage that the adult can begin to play alongside the child and use appropriate questioning to support and further extend play.

In the final stage of the Continuum, the adult selects the activity (again based on observed interest) and the child takes the lead in developing and shaping the direction and nature of play. As children move through the Continuum, the fluid balance between adult and child has almost dance-like qualities. Much like a conversation between equals, the delicate balance between adult and child initiation and consequent enrichment of play, are apparent.

Activity

Follow the different stages of the Continuum (set out on page 36), noticing how your role changes at each stage, and which elements remain constant. Think about other types of play that you observe, support or actively participate in, and for each of these reflect upon your evolving role.

'Young children have a real affinity with the natural world, an insatiable curiosity and a sense of wonder about the tiniest details' (Danks and Schofield, 2005). Given the opportunity, children will discover wonder, excitement and enrichment everywhere from a muddy puddle, to a cool shady spot beneath a tree, or in the cosy indoors. This book gives a mere taster from the feast of sensory-rich play available. It seeks to tantalise the sensory tastebuds and excite and inspire fun. Above all it offers a fresh perspective on something that is often taken for granted or marginalised as messy play. It invites reflection of our own attitudes, a learning journey which I have enjoyed taking in rediscovering sensory-rich play myself. To restrict, segregate (by age) and prescribe would be at odds with

the very essence of sensory play itself. Depending upon the environment and the individual, sensory play can provide a highly motivating, exciting and uplifting stimuli or a deeply calming experience. These ever-changing qualities of sensory play: its open-endedness and ability to inspire awe explain much of the appeal of sensory play. Care does need to be taken however that the instinctive appeal of sensory play does not trivialise its importance, as our senses are ultimately the gateway to all learning. Like sensory play itself, use this book as a resource to dip into, inspire and act as a springboard for your own creativity. In a world where sensory-rich play opportunities are all around, the writing is literally in the sand, so seize the moment, watch children, who are after all the experts, and get playing!

Ayres, A.J. (1972) *Sensory Integration and Learning Disorders*, Western Psychological Services, Los Angeles.

Barton, J. & Pretty, J. (2010) What is the Best Dose of Nature and Green Exercise for Improving Mental Health? A Multi-Study Analysis. *Environmental Science & Technology 2010*. 44 (10), pp. 3947–3955.

Bishop (2006). In: Nutbrown, C. (2006) *Threads of Thinking*, 3rd edition, Sage, London.

Bogdashina, O. (2003) *Sensory Perceptual issues in Autism and Asperger Syndrome (Different Sensory Experiences, Different Perceptual Worlds)*, Jessica Kingsley Publishers, London.

Brierely, J. (1994) *Give Me a Child Until He Is Seven – Brain Studies & Early Childhood Education*, Falmer Press, London.

Chilvers, D. (2011). In: White, J. *Outdoor Provision in the Early Years*, Sage Publications, London.

Cobb, E. (1977) *The Ecology of Imagination in Childhood*, Columbia University Press, New York.

Crowe, B. (1983) *Play is a Feeling*, Unwin Paperbacks, London.

Danks, F., Schofield, J. (2005) *Nature's Playground*, Frances Lincoln Ltd, London.

Department for Education (2011) *Statutory Framework for the Early Years Foundation Stage* (Draft for Consultation, 6 July 2011). [Internet]. (Available from: http://www.education.gov.uk/consultations/index.cfm?action= consultationDetails&external=no&consultationId= 1747&menu=1).

DFE (2012) Statutory Framework for the Early Years Foundation Stage (EYFS), DFE, London.

Dodds, S. (2009). In: Brock, A., Dodds, S., Jarvis, P., Olusoga, Y. (2009) *Perspectives on Play Learning for life*, Pearson Educational Ltd, Essex.

ESRC, Howard-Jones, P. (2007) *Neuroscience and Education: Issues and opportunities*. Institute of Cognitive Neuroscience, University College London.

Fleisher, M. (2001) Autism: An insider view in Richer, J. & Coates, S *Autism: The Search for Coherence*, Jessica Kingsley, London.

Forbes, R. (2004) *Beginning to Play*, Open University Press, Glasgow.

Gascoyne, S. (2010) Sensory Play: An Idea to Treasure, *Practical Pre-School* magazine. January 2010 (108), pp. 16-18.

Gascoyne, S. (2010) Watching, listening and learning from children's sensory play experiences. In: 2010 E*ECERA Conference*, Birmingham, UK.

Gibson, J. (1979) T*he Ecological Approach to Visual Perception*, Laurence Erlbaum, Hillsdale, NJ.

Goldschmied, E., Jackson, S. (1994), *People Under Three – Young Children in Day Care*, Routledge, London.

Grandin, T. in Bogdashina, O. (2003) Sensory Perceptual issues. In *Autism and Asperger Syndrome (Different Sensory Experiences, Different Perceptual Worlds)*, p13, Jessica Kingsley Publishers, London.

Hannaford, C. (1995) *Smart Moves – Why Learning Is Not All In Your Head*, Great Ocean Publishers, North Carolina.

Hill, J. (2010) What influence can regular, unstructured, wild, outdoor experiences have on children with additional needs? In: *Proceedings of the 2010 EECERA conference*. Birmingham, England.

Hughes, A. (2006) *Developing Play for the Under 3s*, David Fulton London.

Kuo, F.E. & Taylor, A.F. A Potential Natural Treatment for Attention-Deficit/Hyperactivity Disorder: Evidence From a National Study American. *Journal of Public Health*. September 2004, 94, pp. 1580-1586.

Louv, R. (2005) *Last Child in the Woods: Saving Our Children from Nature-Deficit Disorder*. North Carolina, Algonquin Books.

Macyntyre, C. (2005) *Identifying Additional Learning Needs*, Routledge, London.

Macyntyre, C. (2010) *Play for Children with Special Needs*. 2nd edition, David Fulton, Oxon.

Mooney, C.G. (2000) *An Introduction to Dewey, Montessori, Erikson, Piaget & Vygotsky*, Redleaf Press, Minnesota.

Palmer, S. (2010) *Modern Childhood*, Out to Play Blog [Internet]. (Available from: http://www.suepalmer.co.uk).

Palmer, S. (2011) Out to Play Blog [Internet]. (Available from: http://www.suepalmer.co.uk).

Peters, T. in Bogdashina, O. (2003) Sensory Perceptual issues. In *Autism and Asperger Syndrome (Different Sensory Experiences, Different Perceptual Worlds)*, Jessica Kingsley Publishers, London.

Play England (2011), *A World Without Play* [Internet]. (Available from: http://www.playengland.org.uk/media/277657/a%20 world%20without%20play-an-expert-view.pdf).

Pound, L. (2006) *How Children Learn*, Practical Pre-School Books, London.

Riedman, S. R. (1962) *The World Through Your Senses*, Abelard-Schuman, New York.

Siraj Blatchford, I., Sylva, K. (2004) Early Years, Thinking Skills, Researching Pedagogy in English Pre-schools. *British Educational Research Journal*. 30 (5), pp.713-730.

Stevens, J. (2006) Dig Deep! *Nursery World*. 12 January 2006 [Internet]. (Available from: http://www.nurseryworld.co.uk/ news/723092/Dig-deep/).

Stroh, K., Robinson, T. & Proctor, A. (2008) *Every Child Can Learn*, Sage Publications, London.

Tickell, C. (2011), *The Early Years: Foundations for Life, Health and Learning. An Independent Report on the Early Years Foundation Stage to Her Majesty's Government*, Department for Education, London.

Tomkins, S., Tunnicliffe, S. (2007). Nature Tables. *Journal of Biological Education*. 41 (4) Autumn 2007. Homerton College, University of Cambridge and The Institute of Education, University of London.

Usher, W. (2010) *Sensory Play Resource Book*, KIDS, London.

Vygotsky, L.S. (Cole M. V. et al. ed.) (1978) *Mind in Society: The Development of Higher Psychological Processes*, Harvard University Press, Cambridge, Massachusetts.

Wartik, N. & Carlson-Finnerty, L. (1993) *Memory and Learning*, Chelsea House Publishers, New York.

White J. (2011) *Outdoor Provision in the Early Years*, Sage Publications, London.

Wilbarger, P., Wilbarger, J. (1991) *Sensory Defensiveness in Children Aged 2-12: An intervention guide for parents and other caregivers*, Avanti Educational Programmes, Denver, Colorado.

Williams, D. (1996) *Autism: An Inside – Out Approach*, Jessica Kingsley Publishers, London.